Juneau

tka

Ketchikan

Port Simpson

ALASKA
CANADA

Nootka

THE GRAVEYARD

Vancouver

Victoria
Seattle

CANADA
USA

Grays
Harbor

D1220217

S O S NORTH PACIFIC

Gordon Newell and his wife, Bonita, afloat on Puget Sound.

Like most professional writers, Newell has been many things—school teacher, newspaper columnist, public relations man, sergeant of Washington State police, and Army officer, to name only a few. His main interest, though, has always been the sea coast and inland waterways of the Pacific Northwest and the ships that sail them.

S O S
North Pacific

Tales of
Shipwrecks off the
Washington, British Columbia
and Alaska Coasts

By

Gordon R. Newell

BINFORDS & MORT, Publishers
PORTLAND, OREGON

Printed and bound in the United States of America
by
Metropolitan Press, Portland, Oregon

TO MY WIFE
BONITA

FERDINAND MAGELLAN, that renegade Portuguese skipper who first sailed across the Great Western Ocean, was an optimist. Only an optimist would have undertaken the first voyage around the world in those five cranky little pumpkinseed boats. Furthermore, only an optimist would have given that mighty sea the misleading name it has carried ever since—the Pacific.

The sun was probably shining, the waters blue and placid, when Magellan sailed into that bright new ocean after his month-long struggle around the foot of South America and through the straits that still bear his name. At such times the western ocean does have a benevolent, pacific air about it; but, all in all, a dangerously misleading air.

It can be voluptuously lazy, beautiful and smiling; an altogether charming wench. But in the wink of an eye

storm clouds can gather. The mild blue sky then suddenly becomes an ominous dark-gray pall. Gentle breezes fly
before the shrieking storm harpies. The ocean rages and
bellows as it sends huge foaming graybeards spouting
against the offshore reefs and frowning headlands. *Pacific*
is an ironic name for this giant sea when winter storms
sweep in to fling themselves against the west coast of
America.

Across the Pacific from the Orient courses a great river
of this sea, the Japanese Current. On reaching the American Coast it is deflected northward, moving inexorably
up the coasts of Oregon and Washington until it meets
its final obstruction—the Graveyard. The *Graveyard*[1]
is the sailors' name for the west coast of Vancouver Island,
which lies off the main body of Canada to receive the full
force of the Japanese Current. Many seamen have found
that the ocean can get even rougher southwest of Vancouver Island than in the neighborhood of the fearful Horn
itself. The wild, lonely beaches of the Island Graveyard
become the last resting place for most of the strange
flotsam and jetsam of the ocean's arterial stream.

Magellan did not live to get really well acquainted
with his Pacific. He was killed by natives in the Philippines
during his first cruise on the sea he named. It remained
for later explorers and merchant seamen to discover
just how unpacific this ocean can be. Oriental junk and
sampan crews probably knew about it long before 1519,
when Magellan took his little fleet across this unknown
sea.

Northwest Indian legends tell of Oriental ships drifting ashore on tribal beaches in prehistoric times. Spanish
galleons, up from Mexico, were the next to feel the
teeth of the northwest Pacific Ocean. Indian legends also
tell of these strange, tall ships wallowing in through the

1.—Another famous Graveyard of the North Pacific is the Columbia River
Bar, where treacherous cross-currents have claimed hundreds of sturdy
vessels.

breakers to pile ashore along the desolate beaches. Sometimes a few pale-faced men with black hair on their chins would come in alive with the wrecked ships. As tribal slaves these men were valuable, for they taught the Indians how to make iron implements and other skills known only to the *Tlo-hon-nipts*—those who drift in from the ocean. Beeswax, the ancient cargo of some lost Spanish galleon, was dug from the Nehalem sands of northern Oregon for generations, first by Indians and then by white settlers.

Though ships were wrecked on the North Pacific Coast ages before historians came to record their fate, their toll became much greater when the first trading ships began voyaging there after the American Revolution. As the land was settled and fleets of merchant vessels visited western ports, the list grew still longer. In the days of sail, the North Pacific claimed the largest toll, for a windship fell easy prey to the stern lee shore with its few safe harbors and its relentless offshore drift. Later, steamers gave the treacherous sea a harder fight, but many of them were also lost.

Even in this day of high-powered ships, of radio and radar and electronic shore beacons, of fast offshore coast guard cutters and far-sweeping rescue planes, the dangerous North Pacific continues to claim occasional ships and men. No ocean is really pacific or really safe, and this is particularly true of the Pacific in its northern reaches.

Sometimes the great storms blow in across the foaming beaches at more than a hundred miles an hour. Gales of sixty miles an hour and more are common during the winter months. These winter storms were deadly to the old-time windjammers that came to the Columbia River for wheat, to Puget Sound for lumber, or to British Columbia for canned salmon. Usually only the wreckage on the Graveyard told the brief story of their fate.

The case of the British bark *Endora* will give some

idea of the fury of a typical North Pacific winter storm. Late in November of 1912, that big offshore windship came booming up over the horizon to make her landfall at the northwest corner of Washington—Cape Flattery. When her lookout sighted the cape, she was just eighteen days out from the Hawaiian Islands. Her voyage should have been almost over then, for she was only a hundred miles or so from her Seattle dock. But it was twenty-four days after that first sight of Flattery when the bark clawed past the cape to safety in the straits.

Before he got his ship to inland waters, Captain Atkinson, the *Endora's* master, was a frustrated man, but he was no more frustrated than many earlier and later windship masters. Atkinson had intended to bring his ship in smartly with a brisk west wind until she was inshore from the lightship and almost ready to ease around the cape. But the westerly suddenly became a screeching southeast gale, sending the unhappy ship careening back out to sea again. Six times the *Endora* sighted Cape Flattery. Six times the devilish southeast gale drove her back over the horizon. On the seventh try she made it. After her landfall it took her nearly a week longer to get into the harbor than it had required to make the entire passage from Honolulu.

The Captain put the final stopper on Magellan's optimism when he said:

"Talk about Cape Horn! The weather we got off Flattery was as bad as anything that will happen off the Horn!"

Every mile of the rugged coastline of Oregon, Washington, British Columbia and Alaska has had its quota of tragedy and high adventure in the age-old struggle of men against the sea. By taking any ten-mile stretch of northern beach and telling what has happened there, a volume of sea lore could be written. The stories that follow here are less limited as to locale, but generally they have been kept within certain geographic boundaries. There are tales of shipwrecks on the northern seacoast of Washington, from Grays Harbor to Cape Flattery. At Flattery the course divides—north and east along the shores of the Graveyard, Vancouver Island, and east through the Straits of Juan de Fuca.

At Dungeness, where the shore-going waters of the Pacific become officially the inland sea of Puget Sound, the course again separates. It goes south to the sheltered, island-dotted waters of the Sound; and north through the Strait of Georgia between Vancouver Island and the Canadian mainland, through the beautiful, sinister Inland Passage of Alaska to Skagway, at the northern tip of Lynn Canal.

No attempt has been made here to chronicle all the thousands of shipwrecks, great and small, which have occurred in these waters. Nor are these tales confined to the most horrible or the costliest shipwrecks of the Northwest Coast. Not all shipwrecks are horrible or even costly. Some are fun, and some are just plain funny. It is no more possible to portray the real story of the shipwrecks of the Northwest Coast by dwelling only on the tragic and dreadful than it is to tell the story of a human being by recounting nothing but the disasters that befall him.

It is true that great steamships died, carrying hundreds of helpless victims to awful death with them; that tall, lovely windships drove ashore in splintered ruin or went missing with all hands. But it is also true that other ships indulged in tranquil, charming shipwrecks that delighted their passengers and caused only minor inconvenience to their crews.

Some ships even proved their human traits by getting themselves into ludicrous and undignified shipwrecks that embarrassed rather than endangered their crews. One stately Cape Horn square-rigger collided with a Seattle dray-horse. . . . There must be a bit of good humor, a few chuckles, in any real tale of the sea. It is hoped that in these stories you will find the laughter along with the drama and the tragedy of the shipwrecks of the Northwest Coast.

CONTENTS

CONTENTS—Continued

MANY BOLD SKIPPERS
had stretched their canvas up the cold, windward reaches
of the North Pacific before Robert Gray and George Vancouver voyaged there. But Fame reserved special honor
for them. To Gray went the glory of discovery of the
mighty Columbia River; to Vancouver, discovery of the
great inland sea of Puget Sound as well as the first clear
charting of both of these vast bodies of water.

Within a handful of years following their explorations,
a sizable fleet of square-rigged ships and rakish brigan-
tines was trading regularly to the Columbia and to Puget
and Nootka sounds. Great Britain and New England vied
in their search for rich, new fur markets, even though torture and death rather than gold often awaited these sailor
traders. The first well-documented marine disaster in
Pacific Northwest waters, and one of the grimmest, oc-

1

curred in Nootka Sound, five miles above Friendly Cove, the location of the ancient Indian village of Uquot.

The full-rigged ship *Boston*—out of Boston by way of Hull, England—arrived at Nootka on March 12, 1803. She was typical of the pioneer trading fleet. In her home port she had stowed a cargo of trade goods: bright-hued cloths and blankets, twenty hogsheads of black trade rum, cutlasses, pistols, muskets and fowling pieces, blackstrap molasses and brown sugar; along with such gewgaws as tin mirrors, beads, cheap knives, and razors. With such cargo Captain John Salter expected to seduce the savage hearts of the Northwest Indians and pick up a profitable load of prime furs.

As the *Boston* rode at anchor on the morning of the second day, Chief Maquina and a number of his braves paid a visit to the Captain. Gifts were exchanged, including an engraved, double-barreled shotgun for the Chief. That afternoon many more natives came aboard and stood in open-mouthed admiration of the marvelous cargo. Taking advantage of the childish intellects of the savages, the seamen drove sharp bargains; mere trinkets were traded for prime furs. Brisk trading continued for almost a week. It looked as if the *Boston* would complete a profitable voyage and even add new lustre to the existing friendship between the Yankee traders and the Northwest Indians.

On the morning of the nineteenth of March, Maquina came aboard with a brace of ducks. Despite his gift, he was hotly indignant. The new gun was unsatisfactory. He pointed to a broken lock. Now, coast Indian dialects were not lauguages of diplomacy, nor were they designed to convey fine shades of meaning. As far as the old Chief was concerned, the fancy Boston gun was *peshak*—no good— and he meant to have something done about it. Maquina had learned profound respect for the white man's firearms, and he wanted the best.

Captain Salter's ruddy face purpled with rage as the

Chief ranted. He had wasted a fine fowling piece on this savage and was getting only trouble for his kindness. Snatching the gun from Maquina, he flung it down the open companionway. Further to relieve his boiler pressure, he cursed the savage with all the fluency and originality of an old-time, down-East windship master. Unfortunately Maquina had heard a number of the Captain's expressions before. Like most primitive people in touch with Americans for the first time, the Indians had picked up a fair smattering of cuss words. So, while the Chief knew little other English, he had a pretty good idea of what the Captain was saying about him, his ancestors, and his tribe in general. With the offended dignity of a Roman emperor, he drew his otter cape around his shoulders, beckoned to his scowling braves and departed.

Concerned at this show of hostility, the ship's officers ordered that no more Indians be allowed on deck unless they left their weapons in their canoes. As nothing serious seemed to develop, trading was resumed in a few days. Once again the big cedar dugouts brought out loads of dried salmon to add to the *Boston's* stores for the return voyage. On the day before she was to sail, Maquina in his war canoe appeared off the quarterdeck and suggested that Indians and whites forget their little differences in a farewell celebration.

Indians were allowed aboard, without their weapons, and were doled out an issue of rum. For entertainment, some of the more gifted crewmen performed hornpipes and breakdowns. The savages reciprocated by donning paint and feathers for a friendly war dance around the mainmast. During the festivities Chief Maquina's friendly courtesy won him an invitation to dine in the cabin with the ship's officers.

After dinner most of the crew remained on deck to swap tobacco and odds and ends of nails and twine for Indian curios to take home to Boston. Sailmaker John Thompson was forward in the sail locker checking his stores in preparation for the morrow's sailing. Armorer John Jewitt had gone below to clean muskets. Engrossed in his work, Jewitt was startled by sudden outcries and a great commotion on deck. He hurried up the companionway to see what was going on but had time for only a split second's glimpse of blood-spattered decks. As his head rose from the companionway, a painted savage grasped his hair and lowered a hatchet in the direction of his skull. The armorer's short-cropped hair saved him. The Indian lost his hold on it and Jewitt, falling away from the blow, sprawled back down the stairs. There he lay unconscious in a widening pool of blood.

Weapons had been smuggled to the braves by the many squaws who came aboard later. At a signal from Maquina the braves had attacked the unwary crew of the *Boston.* They had avenged Captain Salter's insult to their Chief.

When Jewitt finally came to, he heard the guttural voices of Maquina and others through the closed door of the companionway. He understood they planned his death, and, knowing something of Indian customs, he regretted that the hatchet had not gone deep enough to grant him a quick death. Again he drifted into unconsciousness. On next opening his eyes he discovered he had been carried to the deck. Bending over him was the old Chief. Abruptly Jewitt was given a choice of death or slavery. In answer he kissed Maquina's feet.

Despite the family gunlock, Maquina still had high regard for the white man's weapons and he valued Jewitt's skill in making and repairing guns and cutlasses. He could keep him as a tribal slave and weapons maker. So the armorer was led to the afterdeck. Savages crowded around Jewitt but at first he saw not a single white man. Then, as his eyes focused better, he discovered his shipmates, or what was left of them. In a double row along the bulwarks sat their severed heads, each resting in a neat crimson circle on the white planks. The armorer's stomach heaved. Quickly he looked away.

Those pale, distorted faces both fascinated and repelled him. He looked at them again. He counted them. There were twenty-five. Including himself, the *Boston* had carried a crew of twenty-seven. Apparently someone else had escaped. As the heads rested there in precise formation, Jewitt mentally called the roll of his shipmates: Captain John Salter, First Mate Delouisa, Second Mate William Ingraham. Next in order was the big, close-cropped head of Boatswain Edward Thompson, then the pinched features of his blacksmith friend John Dorthy and the mutilated face of Samuel Wood, the Scotsman. The dark features of Jupiter Senegal, the giant negro seaman, and of John Wilson, the colored steward—gray now in death— were easily identifiable. When he had checked off the long roll, John Jewitt found that only Sailmaker John Thompson was missing from the gruesome last muster of the ship's company.

Suddenly shrill whoops sounded from the hold. A number of warriors emerged, dragging Thompson. At a sign from Maquina one of the braves drew a knife and grasped the sailmaker firmly by the hair. Sick and shaken, Jewitt staggered to the Chief's side. Using signs and shreds of the Indian and English tongues, he pleaded for the life of his one remaining shipmate. Obsessed with the desire to save his fellow white man, he had a flash of inspiration. Thompson was old and he himself was young. Why not pretend Thompson was his father? Turning to Maquina he asked, "You would not kill my father, would you?" The ruse worked. Probably the Chief remembered his great love for his own handsome son, young Sat-sat-sok-sis.

On the following day Thompson and Jewitt, following orders, drove the ship close to the shore directly in front of the village. There the Indians began their systematic looting. Sails were cut loose, yardarms chopped off, and lines pulled down. Maquina ordered one of the ship's cannons carried to the beach and set up where it would command the entrance to Nootka Sound. The Indians had already heaped the beach with goods from the ship's hold when they came upon some unbroached hogsheads of rum. Visiting members from a neighboring tribe shared the ensuing screeching, drink-maddened night. Torchlight and drumbeat made weird contrast to the high, shadowed hills rising beyond the village.

Near midnight of the second day of revel, Jewitt was awakened by a terrific explosion in the direction of the *Boston*. A second blast seemed to hurl the entire ship clear of the water. Fire burst from the belly of the brig, ripped her wide open, and hurtled her timbers through a briefly-lighted sky. . . . A drunken brave, probably in search of more rum, had set off all the powder that remained in the ship's magazine.

For twenty-eight months Jewitt and Thompson lived with the Indians of Nootka. The armorer, whose quick wits had saved the sailmaker's life, soon learned the Indian language and was generally accepted by the tribe, but the hot-tempered Thompson did not fare so well. In time, Maquina arranged a marriage for Jewitt with a Haida princess, a beautiful daughter of a Queen Charlotte Island chief. Since even by white standards, many of the Haida maidens were very lovely, the lonely seaman was probably glad to follow Maquina's orders. Later Jewitt had his bride return to her people, carrying letters which she was to give to all white men she met. These letters urged the rescue of her husband and Thompson. In his *Narrative*[1] of those days, Jewitt states that it was actually Mackee Ulatilla, chief of Klaiz-zart, who delivered his message to Captain Hill of the armed Boston trading brig *Lydia*.

In mid-July, 1805, Captain Hill, with guns run out and boarding-nets rigged, put into Nootka Sound. Maquina was forced to bring to the brig his two prized slaves

1.—Jewitt kept a journal of his years of captivity at Nootka. On his return home he wrote a book from this record. It became a best-seller and made the fate of the *Boston* go down in history in all its authentic, lurid detail. *Rivers of Rain* by Thomas M. Aumack is based in large part on this book.

as well as what remained of the stores from the *Boston*. Cannon, cloth, guns, and blankets were quickly swung aboard to be eventually returned to the New England owners of the scuttled ship.

During the century and a half that has elapsed since these events at Nootka Sound, many changes have taken place in that small harbor.[2] The loud throbbing of drums no longer rouses the Uquot warrior to battle. Greedy brave and squaw gorge no more on salmon spawn at great potlatches. Uquot is now in ruins, the villagers having long ago left to work in canneries and live in company shacks. Around the weather-beaten and deserted dwellings lean numerous decaying totem poles. Several of these are still in the building where formerly tribal council was held.

Of the *Boston* massacre itself there remains a mute and grim reminder. A short distance from the beach and hidden by heavy woods is the old ship's cannon that Chief Maquina had ordered set up on the beach of Friendly Cove to command the entrance to Nootka Sound.

2.—While gathering material for his book, Mr. Aumack visited Nootka Sound and had many talks with the old Indian lighthouse keeper, who showed him around the ancient village.

CAPTAIN JONATHAN THORN of the American armed merchant ship *Tonquin* was a man who, for pure cussedness, loomed head and shoulders above his contemporaries in an age when shipmasters were seldom noted for their kindly natures. The *Tonquin*, his last command, was a staunch ship of some three hundred tons, carrying an armament of ten carronades and a crew of twenty men. John Jacob Astor's Pacific Fur Company owned her and, late in 1810, dispatched her under Captain Thorn to establish a fur post near the mouth of the Columbia River.

Captain Thorn seemed cut out for the job. He was a regular navy officer, noted as a disciplinarian, the kind who felt the service had gone to the dogs when they abolished keelhauling. Astor finally wangled leave for him from the Navy Department.

The U. S. Frigate *Constitution* escorted the *Tonquin* down the Atlantic Coast, just in case a prowling British

8

warship should be tempted to try her pressgang tricks on one of Astor's ships. Even then, rumblings of discord were beginning to be heard aboard the *Tonquin*. A number of Scottish and French-Canadian fur traders and factors, shipping as passengers and all rugged individuals, did not relish Captain Thorn's iron-handed rule. The merchant seamen of the crew feeling the same way, the gratings were rigged almost daily for punishment. Few of the seamen escaped a bitter taste of the cat. Passengers and crew alike soon dubbed the *Tonquin* an out-and-out hellship. By the time she had reached Honolulu, mutiny and murder threatened.

In the South Seas, as the *Tonquin* lay becalmed, some of the fur traders took a ship's boat to visit a nearby island. A good wind suddenly springing up, Captain Thorn sailed away without them. Luckily the wind failed and the traders regained the ship after hours of hard rowing. The experience did not improve their relations with the surly and arrogant Captain.

Twenty-three days out from the Sandwich Islands, the *Tonquin* reached the mouth of the Columbia River. The bar was breaking in a great welter of dirty, gray-white surf, lashed by a sweeping gale. In later years the mighty river has been partly tamed by massive jetties and deep-sea dredgings, lighthouses, buoys, and a lightship; but in those days nothing checked the seething maelstrom of broken water where the tremendous current of the river met the storm-whipped fury of the ocean. Nothing marked the shallow, ever-shifting channels. No lifesaving crews came to the aid of lost ships; only the stolid Clallam Indians watched hopefully from the beach. Wrecked ships meant good beachcombing.

A wiser sea captain would have waited, well offshore, until the Columbia Bar was in gentler mood, but not Captain Thorn. He ordered the mate and seven seamen to man the whaleboat and pilot the *Tonquin* over the bar.

The whaleboat was rotten and leaky. Mate William Fox pointed this out to the Captain. Thorn shouted:

"If you are afraid of the sea, Mr. Fox, you should never have left Boston!"

At this insult, Fox and the others climbed into the whaleboat and went over the side into the boiling surf. For a few moments they drifted wildly toward the spouting bar, then were blotted from sight by a great, sweeping roller. The boat never came up, nor was any of its crew ever seen alive again. The *Tonquin* lay at anchor till morning, when one of Astor's Scots put out in the pinnace for another try at sounding the channel. This boat also was swamped, the men in it barely escaping.

By now the ship had dragged perilously near the beach. Something had to be done quickly. Supplies for the remote, new settlement included frames for a little schooner, the *Dolly*.[1] The parts were hoisted on deck and the little craft was rapidly assembled, heaved overside, and manned. She found and marked the channel but was swamped on her way back to the *Tonquin*. Ignoring the schooner's crew as they struggled in the surf, the Captain headed his ship toward the channel the *Dolly* had marked for him.

For a time it looked as if the *Tonquin* was going to make it into quiet water without further mishap. Then suddenly she struck a hidden shoal where she stuck fast. Ashore, the Clallams grinned happily as they waited for the sea to bring them its spoils. But the rising tide freed the ship before she was pounded to pieces. She drifted on into the river mouth in front of a southwester and was finally brought to anchor, battered and with tangled rigging and strained spars.

It was now April, 1811, and Duncan McDougal and David Stuart, Astor partners, had selected the site of Astoria during what Thorn termed a "sporting excur-

---

1.—The *Dolly*, the first vessel launched on the Columbia River, was wrecked within an hour of her launching. Only two of her crew were found alive. Later she drifted ashore and was rebuilt.

sion." After discharging the portion of her cargo earmarked for the new post, the *Tonquin* hurried north toward Vancouver Island to trade for a cargo of furs. Entering Clayoquot Bay, she anchored off a large Indian village where the crew carried on lively trade with the natives. In the many years old Chief Nookamis had traded with Boston men he had learned to drive a shrewd bargain. When Thorn discovered that he could not swindle the simple savages as thoroughly as he had hoped, he flew into one of his fine navy rages. During his tantrum he hurled the dignified old Chief overboard. When a sub-chief protested, Thorn had him kicked overside to join Nookamis.

With the entire Indian population by now in a screeching frenzy, the ship's company entreated Thorn to leave Clayoquot and try doing business in some more healthful location. As usual, the Captain refused to listen, taunting all and sundry as lily-livered, yellow-bellied cowards who would run away at the first whoop of a greasy native.

By early next morning the village clamor had died down and a couple of peaceful-looking canoes put out to the ship with the avowed intent of a little trading. The officer of the deck permitted the Indians aboard. They were led by young Shewish, the son of the outraged Nookamis. While the first party diverted the attention of the watch on deck, an armada of war canoes headed out from the beach. Shortly many brightly-painted warriors poured from all directions over the ship's sides.

When Captain Thorn reached the deck, the situation was already serious. Someone suggested to him that it might be wise to get under way immediately. He refused, probably instinctively. By the time he did order the men aloft and the anchor raised, Indians thronged the deck, busily trading huge armloads of prime furs for knives. The crew could not bring themselves to pass up such a profit, so the natives soon had all the knives, and the sailors had quantities of furs. The stage was set for the

Tonquin's final hour of horror. In *Astoria*[2] by Washington Irving, this account is given:

"The anchor was now nearly up, the sails loosed, and the Captain in a loud and peremptory tone ordered the ship to be cleared. In an instant a signal yell was given; it was echoed on every side; knives and war clubs were brandished in every direction, and the savages rushed upon their marked victims. The first that fell was Mr. Lewis, the ship's clerk. He was leaning with folded arms over a bale of blankets engaged in bargaining when he received a deadly stab in the back and fell down the companionway. Mr. McKay, who was seated on the taffrail, sprang to his feet but was instantly knocked down with a war club and flung backward into the sea, where he was dispatched by the women in the canoes.

"In the meantime Captain Thorn made a desperate fight against fearful odds. He was a powerful as well as a resolute man, but he had come upon deck without weapons. Shewish, the young chief, singled him out as his particular prey and rushed upon him at the first outbreak. The Captain had barely time to draw a clasp knife, with one blow of which he laid the young savage dead at his feet. Several of the stoutest followers of Shewish now set upon him; he defended himself vigorously, dealing crippling blows to right and left and strewing the quarterdeck with dead and wounded. His object was to fight his way to the cabin where there were firearms, but he was hemmed in with foes, covered with wounds and faint with loss of blood. For an instant he leaned upon the wheel, when a blow from behind with a war club felled him to the deck, where he was dispatched with knives and thrown overboard.

"While this was transacting upon the quarterdeck a chance medley was going on throughout the ship. The crew fought desperately with knives, handspikes and whatever weapons they could seize upon in a moment of surprise. They were soon overpowered by numbers and mercilessly butchered."

The seven seamen who had been ordered aloft to make sail lowered themselves by the running rigging. Weaponless, they tried to get between the decks. One fell and was instantly slaughtered; a second was fatally stabbed in the

2.—Particulars were derived from the Indian interpreter member of the crew who had been an eyewitness to the tragedy but had taken no active part. Because of his race he had been spared.

back; a third was killed while going down the hatchway. The remaining four escaped to the cabin where they found Lewis, the ship's clerk. "Barricading the cabin door, they broke holes through the companionway, and with the muskets and ammunition on hand opened a brisk fire that soon cleared the deck." Shortly after the Indians departed, the survivors fired the deck guns, destroying many in the escaping canoes. At dawn the *Tonquin* looked deserted. Later some canoes ventured out to the ship. With them was the interpreter. Lewis appeared on deck, invited the Indians aboard, then disappeared. The decks were soon crowded with Indians intent on plunder.

Suddenly there was a terrific explosion—"Arms, legs, and mutilated bodies were blown into the air, and dreadful havoc was made in the surrounding canoes." The interpreter, thrown unhurt into the water, managed to get into one of the canoes. The bay was strewn with shattered canoes, falling fragments of the *Tonquin,* and with Indians, some wildly swimming shoreward, others gasping in the agonies of death.

Upward of one hundred savages were destroyed; scores more were horribly mutilated; many days later human limbs and bodies were still being washed up on the beach at Clayoquot. The ship's clerk had wreaked his terrible revenge. The four seamen in the cabin with him had got away in the longboat and found a hiding place in a small cove. While asleep, they were found by Indians. Their punishment was lingering death by savage torture. Of the ill-fated *Tonquin,* her despotic Captain, and mutinous crew of twenty, only the Indian interpreter survived.

BETWEEN TRAGEDY AND COMEDY
as between g ᴖod and evil, the margin is often slender, and
Time, in her role of destiny, passes final judgment. That
is the way it is with shipwrecks: not all are eventually recorded as disasters. The infant city of Seattle was saved
because a cruising sloop-of-war rammed herself into an unsuspected reef off Bainbridge Island in Puget Sound and
was held up for repairs. This was in December, 1855,
only a month before the aroused Indians under Chief
Leschi were to focus their wrath on this small West
Coast port of around 150 inhabitants.

During all of that year Washington Territory had been
engaged in a particularly fierce Indian War, the coastal
Indians having been at last goaded into determined violence. Distantly aware of all this, the government ordered

14

the *Decatur* to cruise the coast for the protection of settlers. On December 10, three days after Captain Isaac S. Sterrett had draped his ship ungracefully across the reef, he was relieved from command by Captain Guert Gansevoort. The ship's hull was so badly hogged that Gansevoort doubted whether she could be kept afloat. But she did manage to wallow across the Sound to Seattle where she was beached beside Yesler's wharf in that village.

There her topmasts and yards were sent down and her cannon piled on the dock, her hulk careening on the mudflats as helpless and about as sturdy as a stranded jellyfish. Not only was her hull well stove in, but the parts that appeared sound from the outside were actually in no better shape. Built in 1838, the *Decatur's* hull was mostly punk and dry rot, held together by a thin surface layer of brine-preserved solid wood. In this stage of decay she earned her place in Northwest history.

While the Captain and his crew worked day and night to rebuild this maritime disgrace into a self-respecting man-of-war, the Indians from over the mountains gathered in the forests along Lake Washington for a last, desperate attack on Seattle. They had much to gain and not much to lose. If they won, they would have the supplies of the village and the armament of the *Decatur* with which to carry on war.

The first shot fired was a false alarm. Seaman John Drew, attempting to call on an attractive village maiden by way of her window, met sharp resistance. With a shrill scream, the lady smashed down the window sash and caught the ambitious tar abaft the beam, holding him in that position while whatever plans may have been in his head were revised by a charge of buckshot from her little brother's fowling piece. The boy had heard his sister's cry and had come running. This excitement spurred on the efforts of Drew's shipmates who had stuck to more serious business on the beach. They had the *Decatur* proudly afloat in Elliott Bay by the morning of January

19, one week before the attack. Her masts and spars were
in place, her bilge was fairly dry, and her battery frowned
from the open ports. For the first time since her arrival
she looked sinister rather than pathetic.

When an Indian scout brought word that the Indians
planned immediate attack, Captain Gansevoort ordered
his fighting divisions to strategic positions about the town.
Most of the small arms of the *Decatur* had already been
sent to the defense of other parts of the Sound, but the
brass howitzer remained.   This was now taken ashore.
Some of the citizens sought refuge in the blockhouse
though most of them stayed in their homes, reassured by
the *Decatur*. The night passed without alarm but at
breakfast time on the morning of January 26, the Indians
charged down the Lake Trail upon the small village.

It was the ship's shore parties, marines and seamen,
and more particularly her delayed-action howitzer shells
that turned the tide of battle against the Indians. The
shells that *mox poohed*—fired twice—were too much for
the simple redskins. In his spiced account of the siege,
Lieutenant Phelps[1] says that as the first shell went screeching over the village to land in the woods, the braves were
fascinated. Joining hands, they performed a ceremonial
dance around the sputtering projectile, which seemed to
them to be strong medicine. But it was strictly white
men's medicine, for the dance ended abruptly when the
powder-filled shell exploded violently a second time.[2]

1.—Lieutenant T. Stowell Phelps, navigating officer of the Decatur, left the
only firsthand, written account of the battle. This, penned seventeen years
afterwards, indicates that the lieutenant's imagination was superior to his
seamanship.

2.—The last of the *Decatur's* shells delayed its second *pooh* for a number
of years, only to blow up Dexter Horton, one of Seattle's founders and leading
financiers. Fire Chief Gardner Kellogg had saved the "dud" as a souvenir of
the battle, but later he decided to try an experiment in quick stump removal.
Building a brisk fire under a stump, he rolled the historic cannon ball in on
top of the flames.

Banker Horton, out for a walk, stopped to warm his backside at the fire.
He and the shell warmed up at the same time. When the shell *poohed*, the
banker was propelled several yards through the air to land in a bramble
thicket. Nothing but his dignity was seriously damaged.

In the age of sail, big steam tugs like the *Wanderer* towed many great windjammers out to sea.

The lucky *Queen* (ex-*Queen of the Pacific*) figured in several shipwrecks . . . none of them fatal.

The revenue cutter *Grant* was of little help to shipwrecked mariners of the Pacific Northwest, eventually falling victim to the sea she had patrolled.

Ghostlike *Ryo Maru*, a Japanese fishing sampan, was found floating off Cape Flattery in 1927.
Ten whitened skeletons sprawled on her warped planks; two mummified bodies
occupied her cabin.

Here is all that was left of the twin-screw express steamer *Islander*, hauled from Alaskan waters
by treasure seekers a generation after her sinking.

Much legend has grown up around this historic engagement but of these things we are sure: the Indians were beaten off, the Indian war fizzled out shortly afterwards, and the pioneer citizens of Seattle blessed the lucky reef—still marked Decatur Reef on the charts—that interrupted the cruise of the U. S. S. *Decatur* and sent her to their harbor for repairs.

* * *

A somewhat different story is that of the ancient bark *Southern Chief*, but it too has a happy ending. That decrepit old windjammer undoubtedly saved the lives of all her crew by picking the proper place to collapse of advanced senility and general decay.

Built in New England about 1845, the *Southern Chief* made her first voyage to Puget Sound two years later. She put in at Port Townsend on that trip, helping to establish the town's pioneer reputation for having one of the roughest, toughest waterfronts on the Pacific Coast. Hard-bitten skippers and bucko mates were no rarity in the Port Townsend windship fleet,[3] but the officers of the *Southern Chief* seem to have played even rougher than most. At any rate, she put into Townsend Bay minus three seamen who, their shipmates asserted, had been murdered during a difference of opinion involving the captain. In an attempt to have the skipper prosecuted in the courts of Washington Territory, the survivors hired a lawyer.

Details of the legal battle are clouded with the years. In those days, however, foremast hands had few if any legal rights and were highly expendable. It seems probable that their lawyer made a deal with the skipper. Talking over their grievances in a waterfront dive, the

3.—The story is told of one misguided seaman who, to back up his refusal to work more than eight hours a day, flourished a union rule book under a certain master's nose. The early-day martyr to union standards ate the book's front cover right in Port Townsend Harbor. He ate a page a day thereafter until the book was gone. The back cover was digested sowewhere in the vicinity of Cape Horn, the book being thick and the captain determined.

sailors found that the more siwash whiskey they consumed the greater became the rascality of their attorney. Departing, they accosted him on the street, expressing their heartfelt desire to break his lubberly neck and carve out his black heart if he possessed such an organ.

Being a frontier lawyer, he was prepared for any emergency. He quickly and neatly shot three of the sailors dead. With the butt of a gun he clubbed to death the fourth member of the party. The town gave the four unfortunates a nice, quiet funeral and the incident was forgotten, the *Southern Chief* remaining a frequent caller in the harbor for the next thirty-seven years.

By December, 1894, the windjammer was far gone in old age and decay, but she still paid her owners a profit, and sailors' lives were still cheap. Late that month she cleared Tacoma for Adelaide, Australia, with nearly a million feet of lumber stored in her holds and piled high on her rotten deck. When the steam tug *Wanderer* pulled her clear of Cape Flattery, she spread her patched canvas and squared away before a fresh southeaster. Soon the brisk wind grew into a wintry gale in which she wallowed and ducked, groaning horribly and straining at every rotten timber. After a few hours of this the venerable *Chief* collapsed like the wonderful one-hoss shay. All her seams opened to welcome in the Pacific Ocean, her stern quarters fell overboard, and her decks bulged in alarming hummocks, breaking the deckload gripes and tipping over the donkey engine and boiler. Then her steering gear went adrift and her masts fell down.

Fortunately she lay right in the shipping lane some fifty miles southwest of Flattery. Her crew was soon taken off by the barkentine *Skagit*. Having nothing better to do at the moment, the tugs *Richard Holyoke* and *Sea Lion* later went out to see what had become of the derelict. Because she was still more or less above water, they gingerly put lines aboard, stationing a man with an ax to make a quick cut if she started down. To the amazement of the tugboat men, they hauled the battered wreck all the way into Port Townsend Harbor, where they beached her. Or rather they beached the cargo with bits of the *Southern Chief* clinging to it here and there. The ancient wind-jammer had simply crumbled. She may have towed out to sea carrying her cargo, but the cargo came back carrying her.

Even in the individualistic 1890's, the case of the *Chief* was somewhat out of line. The Seattle *Post-Intelligencer* was scathing in its treatment of the maritime antique's owners, reporting on December 27, 1894:

"The wreck of the bark *Southern Chief* was today towed into port by the tugs *Richard Holyoke* and *Sea Lion*. The vessel is the most perfect specimen of decayed marine architecture that ever reached Puget Sound. The seas ripped dozens of planks from the side of the bark, exposing timbers so rotten that they could be picked to pieces with a jackknife. Rust and innumerable bolt holes had perforated the ribs of the bark until they resembled teredo-eaten piles. Shipping men and veteran sailors who had braved the storms of many seas in vessels considered unsafe were astonished at the complete rottenness of the *Southern Chief*. The decayed wooden timbers were hidden by nicely-painted boards.

"That was the condition of the bark when the owners permitted 15 persons to risk their lives and incidentally involve possible loss of a cargo worth $10,000 by going on a deepwater voyage to a foreign port 4,000 miles distant. It must also be remembered that it was only a year or two ago that the vessel was engaged in the San Francisco-Puget Sound coal trade, making voyages that increased the danger tenfold."

By the next day the *Post-Intelligencer's* Port Townsend marine correspondent had got a better look at the amazing remains of the *Chief*. He added more gruesome details in his follow-up story of December 27:

"The more the facts are known concerning the real condition of the bark *Southern Chief* when she went to sea, the greater becomes the censure for those responsible for allowing 15 people to hazard their lives on such a rotten old craft. Before she sailed

from Tacoma the starboard anchor and 40 fathoms of chain were
lost overboard. Then the bark went to sea with only one kedge
anchor weighing about 2,500 pounds, which would not have
held a vessel of her size in a heavy wind or sea. Below the deck
and hidden by thin planking, there was not a sound timber or
rib in the hull. Under these conditions, opinion prevails that
false representations must have been made to the insurance companies or else the cargo would not have been insured."

Though the *Chief* would not have been safe with only
a hold full of pingpong balls, luckily for the crew she was
carrying lumber instead of coal. They were also fortunate
in that she decided to end her days close inshore rather
than in the trackless wastes of the antipodean seas to
which she was bound. Long overdue at Davy Jones's Locker, the *Southern Chief* atoned for her bloody past by
picking the right time and place to go.

FOR MORE THAN HALF A CENTURY
after the *Boston* was captured and driven ashore by the
piratical Indians of Nootka Sound, redskinned buccan-
eers were among the navigational hazards of Pacific
Northwest waters. The first steamer on the Pacific, the
Hudson's Bay Company's *Beaver,* was equipped with a
battery of brass cannon, small arms, and boarding nets to
repel Indian attacks. Even after the Puget Sound country
became fairly civilized, with newspapers, a university,
and regular steamboat service, Indian pirates remained
a real menace.

During the Indian War of 1855-1857, any unprotected
vessel was fair game for marauding savages. This continued to be a seasonal occupation with them for many
years after the close of hostilities. The squat and lazy
canoe Indians of Puget Sound were seldom if ever the cul-
prits. They might steal a ship's best bower anchor—if they

21

got a chance—and trade it to some noble white man for rotgut whiskey, but they were neither violent nor warlike. They were not the type to take the anchor by force and arms.

A different breed were the fierce, proud Haidas of the Queen Charlotte Islands to the north. For generations they had been accustomed to sweep down in their great seagoing war canoes to raid the defenseless natives of Puget Sound. These pillaging expeditions provided sport and a certain amount of killing practice for the Haida warriors, besides paying dividends in loot, slaves, and the more desirable women. The Haidas saw no good reason to discontinue their amiable jaunts after the white men came to the Pacific Northwest. If the opportunity occurred, they were entirely willing to kill and rob the newcomers.

The Puget Sound *Herald* at Steilacoom warned its readers in the spring of 1858 that "The northern Indians . . . those troublesome and unwelcome neighbors" were on the prowl again, adding that a party of Haidas had made an attempt to take the U. S. Surveying Steamer *Fauntleroy* in Birch Bay. The news item concluded with this bit of sage advice: "It becomes the inhabitants to be on their guard."

The wisdom of the *Herald's* counsel was borne out by further flagrant and unlawful deeds on the part of the Haidas, whose contempt for the whites extended even to United States Government ships and Federal reservations. Late in the summer of 1858, a band of the northern raiders landed at the New Dungeness Lighthouse, broke open the storehouse, and got away with all the oil for the lamps, the whitehall boat, and a quantity of sails and other supplies. As keeper Captain Bayling had only one assistant at the station, he wisely barricaded himself in the lighthouse and let the savages depart in peace. He let it be known, though, that if they had dared to attack the lighthouse he would have chastised them severely.

The brig *Swiss Boy,* outbound from Port Orchard to San Francisco, sprang a leak off Cape Flattery and put into Nitinat Lake on the west coast of Vancouver Island. The plan was to beach it for repairs, but the crew found the bay occupied by a large band of Haidas. Like a plague of locusts, several hundred of them swarmed over the little brig, stripping her of all that was movable, including every shred of rigging, the mainmast, the cargo, and the sailors' clothes. The unhappy crew were imprisoned, but managed to escape after a few days. Reaching Victoria, they notified Canadian officials, who dispatched H. M. S. *Satellite* to round up the Indian pirates that had robbed the honest Yankee mariners of their ship and pants. Most of the loot was recovered and the chief of the band with several of his lieutenants was taken to Victoria in chains. There, to their amazement, they were thrown into jail. The Canadian Indians had felt that the "George's Men," as they called the British, would be pleased to have them do away with a "Boston Ship." [1]

Such events convinced the Pacific Northwest skippers of 1858 and 1859 that a canoe full of northern Indians was as potentially dangerous as a lee shore. Within a few weeks the schooner *Blue Wing* had the misfortune to fall afoul of both perils. In her case the Indians proved the more disastrous. Late in December of 1858, a heavy gale tossed the litle *Blue Wing,* inbound from Semiahmoo (today's Blaine) to Steilacoom, ashore on Point Wilson. She was badly damaged but was repaired and refloated.

In January, 1859, she left Steilacoom on another voyage north in company with the *Ellen Marie,* also a little fore-and-after. The two small ships never reached port. After several months had passed it was assumed that they had sunk or been blown ashore on some remote Vancouv-

---

1.—The northwest boundary dispute between Great Britain and the United States was going full blast at that time and relations between the two countries were strained. The Indians were quick to notice this, but British and Americans kept their quarreling in the family and showed a common front because they were greatly outnumbered by the Indians.

er Island beach. But in April of that year a Puget Sound
Indian showed up at Steilacoom with the true story of
the schooner's fate. He said that a small vessel had been
destroyed at Vashon Island and her crew murdered.

An investigation of his story brought out the particulars of the bloody affair. As the *Blue Wing* was drifting
slowly past the wooded shore of the island, a big canoe
came slashing out from a cove, driving fast for the little
ship.   Ten braves and five squaws swarmed over the
schooner's low rail to make short work of the surprised,
unarmed crew. There were no more than four or five
men on the schooner and none of them lasted more than
four or five seconds after the Haidas hit the deck. Then
the Indians quickly tossed bundles of loot from the ship's
blood-stained boards into the big canoe, opened the sea-
cock and departed. Five minutes later the war canoe and
the killers were out of sight in the dark shadows of the
island's tidal forest. The *Blue Wing,* with her dead crew,
slowly settled to the bottom of the Sound.

Later the Haidas fell on the *Ellen Marie,* but her skipper, Captain McHenrie, was armed and the crew more
alert. The Captain fired on the canoe when the Indians
tried to board, killing the pirate leader, Haida Jim.
Though the war canoe swiftly withdrew out of range,
the Captain's victory was short-lived. At midnight the Indians paddled stealthily into the cove where the schooner
had anchored for the night. The Captain and most of the
crew were asleep and the Haidas drifted over the rail as
silently as swooping gulls. A strangled cry or two, the
flash of knives in the starlight, and it was all over. Another load of booty was tossed into the canoe, a jug
of oil was broken on the cockpit deck, and a torch was
flung. The *Ellen Marie* and her crew were disposed of as
neatly and even more completely than the *Blue Wing*
and her cargo of dead men. No Barbary pirates ever did
their work more efficiently than the Indian freebooters
of the Northwest Coast.

The arrival of steam revenue cutters and warships after the Civil War finally put an end to these pirate raids, but not until the majesty of the Federal Government had received a final insult from the savages.

One day the whole crew of the Tatoosh Island Light Station came ashore, announcing that they had resigned. Inquiries brought out their reason. The Indians had taken over the island, declaring with simple dignity that it had always belonged to them and, since the Great White Father had never paid them for it, they considered it still their property. They would make a potlatch house of the *hyas* long house with the great fire on the roof. The white men had better vacate. The white men did, and until the government got the ownership question straightened out —with the aid of a gunboat—Tatoosh Light had the distinction of being the only station of the U. S. Lighthouse Service to be owned and operated by Indian pirates.

AFTER THE PASSAGE of three-quarters of a century the loss of the paddle steamer *Pacific* off Cape Flattery remains one of the most shocking tragedies in the long roll of Northwest shipwrecks. From Alaska to the Golden Gate, the whole seaboard was plunged into mourning as news of the disaster spread. The population was sparse then and communities more closely knit. A large percentage of the homes in Washington Territory and the Canadian Province of British Columbia were touched personally by the tragedy, counting friends and loved ones among those aboard the ship that never made port.

The *Pacific* was a side-wheel steamship of 875 tons burden. She was built at New York in 1851, but had been brought around to the Pacific Coast shortly thereafter.

26

For a brief time she carried passengers between the Isthmus of Panama and California, then she sailed north to Victoria to carry miners to the Fraser River gold diggings during the gold boom. In the 1860's she ran aground near Coffin Rock on the lower Columbia River. She was given up for lost, but a river steamer brought down the city of Portland's new steam fire engine, which pumped her out and made it possible to refloat her. As events turned out, it would have been better to let her fall apart on the river.

No marvel of the shipbuilder's art when she was new, the *Pacific* was worn out and rotten by 1872. In that year she was tied up along the mudflats, where she quietly decayed for another three years. Then, in 1875, another gold rush developed, this time on the Cassair River of British Columbia. Every old hulk that would float was hastily puttied together and strengthened with a good, thick coat of paint. The *Pacific* came out of retirement to join her last gold rush. Placed on the coast run between San Francisco, Puget Sound, and Victoria, she arrived at the British Columbia capital on her first voyage early in April of 1875. The heavy coat of paint covering her rotten timbers must have fooled the waterfront reporters and her prospective passengers. One of the Victoria papers reported her as "newly rebuilt and in excellent condition." Within six months that optimistic report proved badly in error.[1]

On the morning of November 4, 1875, the *Pacific* steamed out of Victoria Harbor to keep her appointment with death. On the bridge was Captain J. D. Howell, late lieutenant in the Confederate Navy, who had accompanied his brother-in-law, Jefferson Davis, to prison and then to exile after the Southern cause was lost. When the

---

1.—There seems to have been a widespread misconception as to the *Pacific's* seaworthiness at that time. Even after she demonstrated her condition by falling apart at sea, people were still convinced that she had been a fine, stout ship. Reporting on the *Pacific* disaster, the Washington *Standard* said: "True, she was an old ship, but by all reports, staunch and seaworthy." Perhaps the steamship company enjoyed the services of an aggressive public relations man.

first bitterness of the post-Civil War era had passed, Howell returned to America to begin a new life on the Pacific Coast. By the time he took command of the *Pacific*, he was a popular and respected West Coast shipmaster.

The *Paddler's* decks were black with passengers; she had picked up thirty-five on Puget Sound and 135 more were waiting on the Victoria dock when she arrived there. As she was preparing to sail, the purser sold at least twenty more tickets to late comers. Bearded miners, just out of the diggings, were still swarming over her rail as the gang-plank was pulled in. All told, more than two hundred passengers and fifty crewmen crowded the steamer's two-hundred-foot hull by the time the last impatient whistle blast sounded and the starting gong clanged in the engine room.

As the *Pacific* cleared the harbor, Chief Engineer Houston disengaged the "johnson-bar" from its socket in the trip shaft and hooked up the eccentric rods to the rocker arms. The side-wheeler's primitive single-cylinder beam engine had to be valved by hand while running under bells, but at half speed or better the massive iron walking-beam relieved the engineer of that task. When the great beam picked up its precise, nodding rhythm, the paddle-buckets at the ship's side beat the water to white foam at the quickening thrust of the ponderous engine. Swinging to starboard, the *Pacific* squared away on her westerly course down the broad, deep Straits of Juan de Fuca toward the open sea.

After the old paddler had left the shelter of the straits to round Cape Flattery, she met a fresh southerly wind and heavy swells. It was certainly no storm, but the wind was dead against the steamer and the seas were rough enough to set her rolling, pitching, and groaning, while her asthmatic engine gained little headway bucking the strong headwind. Watchers at Tatoosh Island Light Station saw the steamer battling for the open sea in the pallid half-light of the November afternoon. The black,

wind-whipped smoke from her tall funnel streaking away
aft to mingle with low-scudding clouds, and the welter of
white water at her bows created an illusion of speed. It
was entirely an illusion, though, for the laboring *Pacific*
was barely making steerage way. It was evening and the
tower lamps were lighted by the time she had clawed
abreast of the rock. At ten o'clock that night she was not
well off shore. From the lofty heights of Tatoosh the dim
glow of her lights could still be seen through the mist and
darkness.

The south wind that held the steamer *Pacific* bucking
and wallowing in sight of the Graveyard's grim lee shore
was a source of considerable satisfaction to Captain
Charles Sawyer of the full-rigged ship *Orpheus,* north
bound from San Francisco to British Columbia, in ballast.
The old Cape-Horner was standing up the coast, running
dead before the wind while Captain Sawyer noted with
some pride that she was reeling off a good twelve knots.
She was close inshore, but, with head yards braced sharp
up by the starboard braces and her main and after yards
square, she could be hauled offshore at a moment's notice
if necessary.

Ten times Captain Sawyer had taken the *Orpheus*
around Cape Horn. On his eleventh trip, as his fine ship
went bowling up the coast in sight of the friendly coast
lights, he had no premonition of disaster. At half past
nine he turned the watch over to the mate and went
below to check the chart. He had left orders with the
mate to keep a sharp watch to starboard, the landward
side, and if the mate saw anything in that direction he
was to "starboard the wheel and keep her head to the
northward, off shore." [2]

2.—In steering a square-rigged ship, the bow of the vessel turns the same way
the steering wheel does — as in steering an automobile. At the order, "Starboard the wheel" or "Hard a'starboard," the helmsman would turn the wheel
to the left, or to port, the ship turning in the same direction. Thus with the
Orpheus moving up the coast with land on the starboard, or right side, such
an order would turn the ship to port, or to left, toward the open sea. Confusing? The Navy thought so too and changed helm orders to a simple,
though unromantic, "Left (or right) rudder."

No sooner had the skipper reached his cabin and pulled out the chart than he heard the mate shout an order to the helmsman, "Hard a'starboard!" Sawyer heard the creak of the tiller ropes and felt the ship heel over as the helm was put down in response to the order. A glance at the telltale compass showed that the ship's head was rapidly coming around to the northwest. On reaching the deck, the mate informed Captain Sawyer that he had sighted Cape Flattery Light off the port bow.

Knowing this to be impossible, the Captain was not long in identifying the light — on the starboard bow now since the windjammer had changed her course — as the masthead lamp of a steamer. He ordered the helmsman to head up into the wind until the *Orpheus* was pointed somewhat south of west, with the after sails aback. This meant that she had almost reversed her course and, except for the roll of the sea, was hove-to and nearly motionless. The Captain could hear the labored beat of the paddle-buckets as the steamer approached, her masthead light arcking across the dark sky a little forward the windship's starboard beam.

The oncoming steamer was the *Pacific,* and as she forged slowly ahead against the wind and sea, Captain Sawyer watched her anxiously through his glasses. There was still plenty of time for her to change her course but if she failed to do so, collision was certain. No one knows exactly what went on aboard the doomed steamer, but her lookout must have failed to sight the wallowing square-rigger until too late. A fine, persistent rain had come up; the night was dark and starless. When the alarm sounded, the engine was stopped, then reversed, and the paddle-buckets responded with a slow, backward roll. Though the *Pacific* was moving slowly at the time of the alarm and her headway was checked still more by reversed paddle-wheels, her momentum was not entirely stopped.

Slowly, lazily, the steamer's bow reared high above the square-rigger's bulwarks as one mournful cry of warning

came from her whistle. Then, almost gently, her bow
came down, glancing from the ship's side. She recoiled,
forged ahead again, and struck the *Orpheus's* main topmast backstays with enough force to smash the ship's
chain plates. A third time she slammed into the square-
rigger, further aft this time, carrying away considerable
gear and leaving the *Orpheus* pretty well smashed up
aloft.

Though the shock of collision had been light, certainly
not serious enough to cause much inconvenience to a seagoing steamer, the ship was in a dangerous position. Her
hull was possibly opened by the steamer's sharp stem, her
spars and rigging tangled, and she was drifting helplessly
before a strong wind toward the Graveyard's jagged rocks.
Captain Sawyer hailed the *Pacific,* asking her to stand by,
but he got no reply. The paddler was soon lost to sight
in the darkness and rain. Nor did the crew of the *Orpheus*
give her much thought as they fell to, unlashing the lifeboats, sounding the holds, and repairing the damage
aloft. They had not seen a soul on the steamer's decks,
and they had heard no sound from her except that one
futile whistle blast.

The windship men soon got their craft under way
again but the steamship *Pacific* made no port that night
or any other. At the moment of impact her strained and
rotten hull opened up like a dropped melon. In a few
minutes a deluge of sea water flooded the engine room
to stop the engine's slow stamping. High above, in its
gallows frame, the dark skeleton of the walking-beam was
still and rigid. The paddle beat had ceased. While the
stunned crew launched one overcrowded boat, the tired
old *Pacific* rolled sluggishly for a few minutes, then lay
over on her side, filled, and sank. At almost the same time
the one lifeboat capsized and went down. A few human
figures struggled a little while in the grip of the icy
North Pacific rollers, then, one by one, sank out of sight.
A few shrill cries, like the plaintive calling of sea birds,

vied for a moment or two with the wailing of the wind. Only a mass of wreckage remained to show that the steamship *Pacific* had passed that way.

On November 7, the American bark *Messenger* reached Victoria from San Francisco. Twenty miles south of Cape Flattery her lookout had sighted a bit of wreckage with a man clinging to it. It was the *Pacific's* pilothouse and a passenger, Henry Jelley, who was weak and almost unconscious after two nights on his precarious raft. Shortly after his rescue he died of exposure. Later the revenue cutter *Oliver Wolcott* came in with one of the *Pacific's* quartermasters, Neil Henley, who was picked up after eighty hours of clinging to a piece of wreckage. He survived the ordeal but no other living person of the *Pacific's* company was ever again seen.

After the two survivors were brought to Victoria there was still hope that others had escaped. But no glad tidings came. Some of the dead washed ashore along the bleak beaches of the Graveyard, and the body of one young girl was found on the shore just below her Victoria home. A weird trick of wind and tide had carried her more than forty miles, past the Cape and the Graveyard and through Juan de Fuca's Straits to within a few yards of the quiet home she had left to board the *Pacific*.

The Victoria *Colonist* expressed the feeling of that time in its editorial of November 9, 1875:

"We have no heart to dwell today on the disaster that has hurried into eternity so many of our fellow citizens. . . . The catastrophe is so far-reaching that scarcely a houshold in Victoria but has lost one or more of its members. . . . In some cases entire families have been swept away."

When it was found that the *Orpheus* had been involved in the *Pacific's* disaster, people at last found a target for their bitterness. Captain Sawyer, who had so blithely watched the good south wind filling his sails as the *Orpheus* sped north, was now a broken man. After the encounter with the *Pacific,* the mate had made another error in identifying lights. A new beacon had been installed on Cape Beale and the mate had thought it was Cape Flattery. As a result, the *Orpheus* piled up on the Island's Graveyard, a total loss, though the crew escaped to shore.

News of the *Pacific's* dreadful fate was almost too much for the old skipper to bear. He was already suffering the blow of having lost his own ship; now he wept brokenly. But he was to face more trouble. He was blamed for the *Pacific's* foundering and was bitterly attacked for not standing by her. Furthermore, he was charged with deliberately running his ship ashore after the accident, and was arrested on that charge.

Sawyer was eventually cleared but he soon retired from the sea, living ashore at Port Townsend, a quiet, melancholy man, for many years. Almost twenty years after the loss of the *Pacific* he was playing a game of whist with a few other old captains. A warm fire, a spot of grog, and good companionship made theirs a snug haven, for outside the wind swooped in from off Cape Flattery while the bell buoy at Point Wilson clanged a brazen dirge as it swung in the grip of the racing tide. It was a night to make an old sailor thankful that he had "swallowed the anchor" and aware of the blessings of life ashore.

But Captain Sawyer gave little heed to the game. Suddenly he assumed a listening attitude, turning unseeing eyes upon his friends.

"There it is again," he whispered. "Can't you hear it?"

The others heard only the moaning of the wind and the distant tolling of the bell buoy over the fire's crackle.

"What is it, Captain? What did you hear?"

"The whistle of the *Pacific!*"

Two decades before, the whistle of the *Pacific*—that one eerie blast in the night—had signaled the death of two ships and hundreds of hapless people. Its ghostly echo sounding in the mind of Captain Sawyer seemed to warn him that now his time had come, for he was seen no more at the captains' snug hearth.

Shortly afterwards his friends were called upon for one final service to their old colleague. They helped carry Captain Sawyer's body to the cemetery on the bluff above the Straits of Juan de Fuca. There the last victim of the *Pacific* disaster was laid to rest, while, down below, the bell buoy clanged a seaman's requiem.

The loss of the *Pacific* was a disaster of the first magnitude. As such it was the subject of pioneer sermons, newspaper editorials, pamphlets, and poems. Surviving is a tiny pamphlet printed at Nanaimo, British Columbia, in 1875, titled "Ode on the Loss of the Steamship *Pacific*," by the Reverend George Mason, M. A., Anglican Rector of St. Paul's Church of Nanaimo. Despite its lugubrious cadence the poem has found a place in the history of the *Pacific* disaster. Lines from it quoted here show how deeply people at that time felt about the tragedy:

"Hush! —did'st thou hear?—was it the death-shriek woke
The midnight slumbers of that silent home?
Hush!—it is nought!—nought but the watch-dog's howl
Of melancholy omen, boding ill;
Or screech of night-bird hooting to the gale
In fiendish mockery of man's distress.
Sleep on, beloved ones! For a while sleep on
And gather up your strength for morning light!

A day of sorrows waits you! . . . the dreadful news
Has reached our shores! has paralyzed the hearts
Of all! Oh! say it is not true! What! lost!
All lost! All! All but one snatch'd from the deep,
A solitary messenger of woe,
Left on the cruel waters to recount
His tale of misery, the fatal crash,
The rush, the panic—accents of despair,—
The infant's wail,—the mother's piercing cry,—
The brave man's fight with death, and chivalry
Unselfish even to his latest gasp.
And now another, rescued from the waves
But to confirm the tidings of their fate,

Pants forth fresh horrors from the awful wreck. . . .
Pitiless ocean! Thou hast done thy worst!
We ask not this of thee,—to hurl us back
In ruthless scorn the forms of those we loved;
Harrowing our souls with hideous spectacle
Of marr'd remains, relinquish'd—but in vain.
Hide them!—Oh! hide beneath thy briny pall
Corruption's spoils until the day of doom!"

THE FEELING that they had seen all this before must have come to shore-side residents in the Point Grenville area on a wind-whipped January morning of 1892. Many of us have experienced that dreamlike sensation, but they had better reason than most. They watched the same shipwreck happen twice.

That is the story of the British barks *Abercorn* and *Ferndale*.

In January, 1888, the three-masted British bark *Abercorn* lifted her tower of canvas over the rim of the world and stood in toward the mouth of the Columbia River. She was deep laden with English cargo for Portland, Oregon. Fog shut down along the coast before a tug could pick her up. She lay becalmed but drifted relentlessly northward, pulled along by the prevailing current that

36

scours the coast from Cape Disappointment to the Grave-yard.

Early in the morning she drove ashore in heavy surf fifteen miles north of Grays Harbor. Her deep draft kept her far out in the line of breakers and her masts went by the board at the shock of the stranding. It is a great wonder that any escaped from her, but three bruised and battered survivors were picked up on the beach. Because no boats could be launched in the pounding surf they fought their way to the beach with only their own strength to support them.

Four years later, fate completed its grim, practical joke. In January, 1892, the three-masted British bark *Ferndale* was wrecked at the same place, in an identical way. The sole difference was in the matter of date. The crews of both ships rest side by side in two common graves near Grays Harbor, while the two British barks lie buried together under the northward shifting sands of the Washington Coast. Probably no two ships ever followed so strangely similar a destiny.

A SHIPWRECK does not have to be a tragedy. Some are exciting, some comic, some merely expensive. Much depends on wind and weather, the state of the tide, and the skill of the officers and crew. If things break right for a ship, she gets off the beach and goes on about her business. Because a majority of the strandings and collisions with reefs and rocks on the part of Pacific Northwest ships have had nonfatal results, they have seldom been featured in print, except briefly in the newspaper shipping pages of their day. The usual books about shipwrecks are such melancholy recitals of doom, disaster, and death that they are enough to scare timid readers off a ferryboat at high noon. At the worst, most shipwrecks, particularly in this age of radio and helicopter, are simply periods of temporary excitement and momentary discomfort. A few of them, even before the

38

advent of these modern gadgets, were fun for everyone
concerned, like the time the *Queen* punctured her hull
off Cormorant Island in British Columbia:

Of course the old *Queen* was always a lucky ship, even
under her somewhat expansive original name, *Queen of
the Pacific*. While no one dictates to the Pacific, that
mighty ocean seemed to take no offense at the steamer's
title and may even have been a little impressed. The
Queen certainly escaped from several close calls. Other
ships had similar things happen to them, but whereas
the *Queen* always emerged triumphant to go steaming
regally on her way, others often died. Sometimes they
took their people with them.

The *Queen of the Pacific* was built at Philadelphia in
1882, an iron passenger liner of 1,700 net tons. The
Pacific Steamship Company brought her to the West
Coast to run between San Francisco and Portland. A year
after her arrival, her career almost ended. Outbound over
the Columbia River Bar, she was caught in a dense fog
and drifted from the channel to ram hard and fast
aground on Clatsop Spit. Many ships have struck there;
few have escaped. Yet the skies smiled on the *Queen* and
so did her ocean.

The usually tumultuous surf was gentle, treating the
Queen with the respect that was her due. A fleet of half
a dozen ocean tugs hauled her off that grim, ships' graveyard. For a long time afterwards the lucky ship ran on
summer excursions between Seattle and Alaska.

In the summer of 1901, she struck a rock near Five
Fingers, Alaska, but her luck held. Again she got off with
a minimum of damage. Three years later she had more
serious trouble. While on a voyage to Puget Sound from
California, she caught fire off the Oregon Coast. Several
lives were lost, but the fire was beaten out and the *Queen*
raced on up the coast to Seattle, her career just well
begun. She remained a famous, beautiful, and respected
ship until just before World War II. At that time she

was sold to the Japanese for her last voyage—across the Pacific to be melted into guns, tanks, and ammunition. Part of the old *Queen* may have returned to Clatsop Spit in the form of hot shrapnel when a Japanese submarine paid the Columbia River an unfriendly visit in 1942. The *Queen's* luck seems to have held even then. Anyhow, whosoever shot it was that the Japanese Navy used, none of the soldiers in the helpless forts along the river entrance were hurt.

The *Queen's* most charming mishap occurred in the placid years between that maiden stranding on Clatsop Spit in 1883 and her hypothetical return to the Oregon Coast in 1942. It was on August 21, 1894, that she swung away from Ocean Dock in Seattle for a late summer excursion to Alaska. The steamer was commanded by Captain James Carroll, a jovial and highly competent seaman, born in Ireland in 1840. At the age of seventeen, he began sailing on the Great Lakes, soon graduating to deepsea windjammers, including the old clipper ship *Swordfish,* the *Swallow* and the *Rattler.* In 1879 he had command of the famous side-wheeler *Great Republic* when a bar pilot ran her ashore on Sand Island in the Columbia River. The chief engineer, William Allison, was a Californian who had worked up from second assistant in the *Queen's* engine room. Both Carroll and Allison were skilled, experienced men. In addition, the Captain was noted for his gallantry and hospitality toward his passengers.[1] These things combined to make the

---

1.—Steamship passengers can be as difficult as any other passengers, but Captain Carroll was only known to blow up once. That was when the passengers on the *Queen* decided they would like to spend a day at a "quaint" little Indian village along the steamer's route. Accordingly they drew up a petition asking the Captain to make an unscheduled overnight stop there, and they chose the prettiest girl on board to deliver it.

The captain read the petition carefully, then gravely returned it. He informed his passengers that the *Queen* was not a sight-seeing hack and that "this steamship is not run by petitions." It was not much of a blowup, but the passengers were made aware that they had been confusing joviality with weakness. Word got around and the passengers never again tried to navigate the *Queen.*

Queen's 1894 brush with disaster pleasant for her passengers. Among these was a peppery and prominent Civil War veteran, General John H. Bryant, who was receiver for the Seattle Coal and Iron Company. Even this old warrior was as happy as a schoolboy about the shipwreck, saying he would not have missed it for the world. Here is the account he gave of it:

"While we were going north one night, the weather was very foggy and the steamer ran on a rock at Gordon Point, on Cormorant Island above the head of Vancouver Island, between Alert Bay and Port Rupert. One of the plates was smashed in, and, the forward compartment filling with water, the steamer stuck there. Next morning all the freight forward was shifted aft, a lot of coal was cast overboard, the anchors were cut loose and placed on floats, and, after two days, the vessel floated. Captain Carroll then ran her into Alert Bay, where he beached her.

"The chief engineer made a diagram of the break, secured one of the reserve plates aboard, and set to work between tides to repair the damage. A number of Indians were employed to assist, while the entire crew was assigned to give undivided attention to the comforts, wants, and pleasures of the passengers. The sailors rowed us about the bay or took us around the country in steam launches. Even fishing tackle was furnished. We visited old missions, attended Indians dances in the evening, and at other times just enjoyed the woods, the wild scenes, and the sea breeze. The weather was delightful.

"When the forward compartments in the vessel filled with water, the ice stock was demolished and, in the course of a day or two, the meat on board was thrown away. But Captain Carroll saw that no one went hungry. He sent up on the Mimish River and bought three fine steers and some sheep. The animals were slaughtered and the larder replenished. After a week at Alert Bay the plate was put in so well that not a drop of water was admitted. The *Queen* then sailed north."

The General had only one complaint to make. It injured his pride and sense of manifest destiny that he had to sail through Canadian waters to get to Alaska. "As an American," he growled, "I think it a bad thing to be compelled to go through another man's garden to get to one's own farm. The country between Alaska and Washington should belong to this country." He added, somewhat grimly, "We'll have a president some day who will attend to this matter."

The General's attitude may not have been reassuring to our Canadian neighbors, yet he had nothing but praise for the *Queen* and her crew. But who would not have been happy during such a shipwreck?—gliding over blue waters, along green, towering shores; hauling fighting salmon from deep water; having crewmen hover about solicitously with tall drinks, tender beefsteaks, and even the offer of steam launches.

The steamship company spared no expense to make this particular shipwreck a pleasure. Even the shore-side dwellers were happy, their pockets jingling with the good dollars paid for fresh beef, provisions, fishing tackle, and launch charters. Here were no crashing billows, no despairing shrieks, no freezing bodies lashed in the rigging. The lucky *Queen* proved that a shipwreck occasionally can be fun, for some.

THE OCEAN IS THE EARTH'S
last great mystery. Though ships have sailed its more than
seven seas for centuries, there are still vast areas of marine
wilderness seldom, if ever, furrowed by a vessel's prow.
And no man knows what lies in the total darkness of the
ultimate depths. It is no wonder, then, that the sea is such
a prolific breeding-place of superstition, of strange legends, and of tales of the supernatural. One of the oldest
sea legends is of the phantom ship that sails eternally
with her crew of dead men — *By skeleton shapes her sails
are furled, and the hand that steers is not of this world.*

Such ghostly ships have sailed the waters of the Pacific
Northwest, some of them riding the eastern sweep of the
great Japan Current half way across the world to be
borne to a final resting place on the Graveyard by the

northward coastal drift. In the enlightened year of 1927 the American transpacific freighter *Margaret Dollar* came upon a ghost ship between the Graveyard and the Cape and brought the disturbing discovery into Seattle Harbor at the end of a towline. Ten months before, the engine of the big Japanese fishing sampan, the *Ryo Maru*, had broken down off the home islands. During that time she had slowly drifted the 4,000 miles and more to the coast of Washington. Her barnacle-encrusted hull trailed long, mourning wreaths of weed; rotted sails and distress signals streamed sadly from her masts; and the dead manned her deck. Ten whitened skeletons sprawled on the warped planks; the mummified bodies of two more crewmen occupied the cabin.

The boarding party from the *Margaret Dollar* listened to the North Pacific wind humming a low dirge in the tattered rigging of the lonely death ship. After stepping carefully around her silent crew, they quickly returned to their living ship. There are more pleasant places to spend one's time than on a ghost ship's deck, surrounded by the moving mystery of the sea. They took back with them a smooth board covered with scrawled Japanese ideographs. On it were listed the names of the twelve dead crewmen of the *Ryo Maru*. At the bottom of the board the captain had written:

"Our last hope is gone. We have no more food. We are lost."

Indian legends tell of a long line of Oriental sailing craft that, in the dim past, drifted ashore from time to time. Recorded history lists seventy-five such strange visitors picked up offshore or found stranded before 1875. It is quite possible that more will come to the Northwest Coast. Marine records show that countless sailing ships, waterlogged and abandoned off the California and Oregon Coasts, have found their way unguided by human hands to a plot in that bleak cemetery of ships on the west coast of Vancouver Island.

It is easy to see how the myths of the Flying Dutchman [1] and the other ghost ships were born. Many a lookout at the bows of a live ship has peered through the scudding mist and rain and felt hair on the back of his neck stand up at the sight of such a derelict on its funeral voyage. Glimpsed dimly in the dark night watches, her sails streaming out sear and tattered, her decks peopled only by darkness and mystery, and with no human hand at the wheel, such a ship was certainly enough to stimulate the germ of superstition that lurks in the minds of all men.

The American bark *Sea King* got the reputation of being haunted not through any disaster but as an aftermath of a great tragedy that did not even occur at sea. In the summer of 1907, the *King* put in to Seattle from San Francisco for a lumber cargo to help rebuild the latter city that had been destroyed by the earthquake and fire of the previous spring. For ballast the windjammer had brought north a cargo of junk and scrap iron. With most of San Francisco in ruins, such cargoes were plentiful there. Apparently the fire-twisted metal had been scooped up by steam shovels just as the earthquake and flames had left it, and been loaded into the *Sea King's* holds.

Though many of the victims of the earthquake were never found, certainly the crew of the *Sea King* had no idea that their ship was carrying some of the unknown dead as ballast. Such was the case, however, for when the cargo of scrap metal was unloaded at Seattle it was found to be occupied by certain gaunt and grinning passengers who had paid no fare and were not entered on the ship's books. Human skeletons came out of the holds along with the iron beams and structural steel that had crushed the

1.—The *Flying Dutchman* is a legendary spectral ship, supposed to be seen in stormy weather off the Cape of Good Hope. It is considered to bring ill-luck. According to Sir Walter Scott, it originally carried a cargo of precious metal but, a horrible murder having been committed aboard, a plague broke out among the crew and no port would allow the vessel to enter. The ill-fated *Dutchman* still wanders about, ghostlike, doomed never more to find harbor.

life out of their victims when the great earthquake struck.
It was prabably just as well for the peace of mind of the old
bark's crewmen that they were unaware of their uninvit-
ed guests, for these could hardly be classed as pleasant or
reassuring shipmates.

After that it was no great strain upon the imaginations
of her crewmen to hear the clanking of rusted iron chains
and the groaning of the unburied dead when the windjammer's timbers creaked to the buffeting of wind and
sea. Some awful fate probably should have befallen the
Sea King as a result of her bad luck in shipping that gruesome cargo, but she pursued an unspectacular, though
haunted, career until the shipbreakers got her.

No one ever actually saw the unknown ghosts of the
Sea King, but a number of people avowed they had seen
and actually conversed with the specter that haunted the
warped decks of the old lumber barge *Rufus E. Wood.*
No one seemed to have a proper explanation for the
supernatural goings-on aboard the haunted barge, but the
Wood had once been a proud and graceful schooner and
the spirit may have been that of one of her former skippers who was so upset about her ignominious fate that he
was unable to rest quietly in his grave.

At any rate, the newspapers of November 23, 1916,
carried such tidbits as the following concerning the un-
rigged vessel *Rufus E. Wood:*

MYSTERIOUS GHOST ON OLD BARGE
TALKS AT SPIRITUALISTIC SEANCE

——

Men Say Spirit of Former Mariner Stalks
Deck of Rufus E. Wood *at Midnight Hour*

Port Angeles recorded: "Mystified at the continuous
appearance of the 'phantom captain' who, through his
midnight walks on the deck of the old lumber barge
Rufus E. Wood, has instilled fear and terror into the

hearts of the sailors, local spiritualists held a seance on the old vessel and called upon the ghost to appear and explain his actions.

"According to the investigators, he came aboard all right and presented a remarkable appearance. Witnesses were taken back to the days when clipper ships were queens of the waters, and they heard a deep bass voice 'piping up the sail.' "

After going on at some length regarding the masculine shade that "piped up the sail" for the edification of the spiritualists, the article concluded that the ghost had been positively identified as that of a "Captain Svenson," a husky Norwegian specter with a luxuriant blond beard and "an unhealed scar on his cheek." When asked to account for his weird and wonderful activities aboard the barge, however, he — or it — went overside and vanished in the chill waters of Port Angeles Harbor.

The spiritualists were convinced that they had met a *bona fide* phantom that paced the deck of the barge *Rufus E. Wood* when the midnight bells tolled, and they planned further meetings aboard the old craft on her future calls at Port Angeles. History does not record the outcome of these. Perhaps the amateur psychic researchers found that some waterfront character with a sense of humor had been pulling their legs. The writer prefers to think of the charming "Captain Svenson" as an authentic seagoing spook. The reader, of course, can draw his own conclusions.

Not exactly a specter bark, but certainly a first-class mystery ship is the strange foreign steamer of the Puget Sound mill port legend. This doomed visitor, flagless and nameless, is said to have put in at one of the sawmill docks on a long-ago day. Though most of the world's nationalities were represented among the mill hands and the crews of the sailing ships at the dock, this crew spoke a language that no one understood. A lovely woman in a red cloak was seen on the bridge of the steamer but only the captain came ashore. He seemed to be under a great mental strain and soon returned to his ship, got her lines in, and headed out to sea. When she was far out in Admiralty Inlet, the mysterious ship suddenly erupted into flames. When a mill tug reached the spot, nothing was discovered but a bit of scorched wreckage floating on the surface. And that was all that was ever found of this strange and ill-fated ship.[1]

1.—From *The Roaring Land* by Archie Binns.

THE STEAMBOAT THAT WOULDN'T STAY WRECKED

BY 1894, A NATION-WIDE DEPRESSION had limped westward to settle drearily on the Northwest Coast. Ships without cargoes sadly swung at anchor or gathered rust along neglected piers while hungry seamen tramped the waterfronts in search of jobs or handouts. That depression clung like a Cape Flattery fog for three years, until July 17, 1897, to be exact. This was the day the Nome steamer *Portland,* down from the mouth of the Yukon, swung into Seattle Harbor to tie up at the old Schwabacker Dock. The *Portland's* cargo was Prosperity.

The news flashed across the nation that the *Portland* had arrived at Seattle from Alaska carrying "a ton of gold" and was coaling up as fast as possible to race back for more. It was really a ton and a half of treasure that she carried, but a Seattle *Post-Intelligencer* writer had coined

49

the "ton of gold" phrase which struck the nation's fancy and sounded the keynote of the great Alaska Gold Rush which was to follow.

Word spread that the *Portland's* strongboxes held only an infinitesimal sample of the incredible treasure of the Klondike, that one of her passengers in a single day had panned $25,000, and that almost a thousand dollars in raw gold had come out of one pan of river gravel. An easterner was said to have taken a hundred thousand dollars from his claim in three months, then to have sold it for more than a million.

After that the waterfronts of the Pacific Northwest roared with action. Thousands of gold seekers thronged the docks demanding passage to the Far North. Mining outfits, sled dogs, gold dredges, roulette wheels, whiskey barrels — mountains of cargo overflowed the warehouses awaiting ship space. As the Alaska ships swung away from the docks crammed with hundreds of adventurers, thousands of others poured in from the East.

Daily more ships joined the golden pilgrimage to the Far North, good seaworthy steamships and graceful windjammers, jaunty little Puget Sound steamboats, and doubtful craft out from long lay-ups in the bone yards. River boats were needed to ply the long route from the mouth of the Yukon River to the inland gold diggings and there were plenty of shallow-draft stern-wheelers eking out a precarious living for their owners on the Sound and its tributary rivers. Many of these set out on the 2,500-mile ocean voyage to the edge of the Arctic Sea. Indicative of the spirit of the times, even the most unseaworthy of these floating coffins never lacked crews or passengers. People were ready to go north on anything that appeared to float.

In 1898, the Canadian Development Company of Victoria, B. C., sent three big river paddlers north — the *Canadian,* the *Columbian* and the *Victorian.* Designed and built to operate on the Yukon, they were typical Pa-

The little "Ships of the Inland Sea"—Puget Sound passenger steamers—were frequent accident victims, but they rarely cost lives.

The Puget Sound stern-wheeler *Multnomah* was rammed by the express steamer *Iroquois*. As in most Northwest inland steamboat sinkings, there was no loss of human life.

The Inside Passage to Alaska is strewn with wrecks like that of the old Pacific Coast Steamsh Company liner *Al Ki* (above) and the more modern motorship *Zapora* (below).

cific Northwest stern-wheelers, a little under 200 feet in length, broad beamed, flat bottomed, and kept from drooping at the ends by heavy steel hog chains running from bow to stern. Though not designed for deep-sea work, they had plenty of it ahead of them before they could start earning money on the Yukon. In front of them lay a voyage of more than 800 miles on the treacherous North Pacific Ocean to Kodiak, followed by another 1,400 miles up the Alaska Coast, through the shallow, dangerous Bering Sea, and on north to the verge of the Arctic Ocean. The only special preparations made for the voyage were the addition of heavy housings of 2-by-12-inch timbers to protect the lower cabins from the ocean rollers, and strongly braced "snowplows" of the same material to help deflect seas from the stern-wheelers' low, blunt bows.

Among those who helped to take the little flotilla of river boats to the Arctic was young Captain Fred G. Lewis, who left the Red Collar boats of the Shaver Transportation Company on the Columbia River to have command of the *Victorian*. Captain Lewis was then a young man but he knew steamboats and had become a marine engineer at the age of eighteen. Nevertheless, as he watched the skipper put on his store clothes to head for the bright spots at the end of each run, he decided he was "working on the wrong end of the boat." Because there was always greasy work to be done in the engine room, even when the boat was tied up between runs, Lewis had master's papers too before he was twenty and had moved from the boiler deck to the pilothouse. He had seen plenty of swift water on the Columbia and its tributaries and enough of the Columbia Bar to know the power of the North Pacific Ocean. When he was offered almost five times the pay he was making on the Columbia to take over the *Victorian,* he figured it was worth a little risk.

The steamboats put out from Victoria Harbor heavy

laden with fuel and supplies. Boiler water was no problem. The sheer mountain coast of Northern British Columbia and Alaska abounds in waterfalls which drop from mountain crests to salt water. In many places, deep water reaches to the very foot of the cliffs. The steamers simply ran alongside the mountains close to a convenient waterfall, got their lines and hoses out, and pumped part of the waterfall into their tanks. This worked fine until the *Victorian's* tanks ran low at an hour when the tide was ebbing. Captain Lewis thought it would be safer to wait for an incoming tide before running alongside the nearest mountain range but one of the other captains, who had been that way before, thought differently. He told Lewis to follow him and he would lead him to a watering spot that was safe at the lowest tide. As time meant much money in this business and the other skipper acted as though he knew what he was talking about, Lewis doubtfully agreed.

The waterfall was there all right, and the other captain took his boat in first to demonstrate how safe it was. Next, Lewis edged the *Victorian* in, got out his lines, and started pumping. But the Alaska Coast has other less pleasant phenomena than a rugged shoreline and graceful cascades; she has many uncharted pinnacle rocks. One of these was lurking unseen, directly under the moored stern-wheeler. As the tanks filled and the tide ebbed, the hull settled lower and lower, ever closer to the hidden rock fang.

When he saw the deck bulging, Captain Lewis leaped to the engine room bell pulls. But he was too late. The *Victorian* had thoroughly impaled herself on the jagged pinnacle and the tide was still going out. The *Canadian* came up to add her power to the end of a towline. It was no use.

As the tide dropped lower, the steamer's full weight came to rest on the sharp rock, the hull slipping down until the rock protruded five feet above the level of the lower deck. At dead, low tide — those waters have a fall of twenty feet or more — Lewis rowed around under his steamer in a skiff. The hull was skewered amidships and she was sitting on an even keel, yet the lowest point of her keel was so far above his head that he could not even touch it when he stood up in the boat and stretched his more-than-six-foot frame as far as he could.

Though it was a disheartening sight for a young captain starting a new career, in another six hours things looked even worse. If too much of the *Victorian* had been showing at low tide, too little of her was visible at high water. The rock refused to relinquish its grip. The water rose until only the funnel, the masts, and the top of the pilot-house could be seen. The other steamers gave up and pushed on north but Lewis would not give up, determined to stay as long as there was anything to be saved. He dispatched a boat crew toward Fort Wrangell to look for a tug and barge to salvage the steamer's machinery, which seemed to be about all that remained worth saving. After the boat left, he noticed the heavy timbers that formed the steamer's seagoing housing. They gave him an idea and he mustered the crew.

"While we're waiting we might as well get busy," said Lewis. "I think we can save the boat."

And that is exactly what they did. The timbers were used to build a cofferdam around the rock embedded in the hull. The tanks were pumped out, the boat lightened, as much as possible, and holes bored to let the sea water out at low tide. Finally, a quick check of the tide tables indicated that an unusually high tide was due. Holes were plugged and the crew stood ready. The lightened steamer rose higher and higher with the incoming flood until at last she floated free, her hull dry and buoyant.

So quickly was the job done that the small boat was picked up before she made it halfway to the nearest tug. Then Captain Lewis put in to Fort Wrangell, hired Indians to help him build a gridiron on the beach, and pulled the *Victorian* out for permanent repairs. He replaced the frame and planking, then took her on to St. Michael, which was where he had been paid to take her.

At St. Michael, a cargo was waiting for the *Victorian*. Lewis got this aboard in a hurry, heading up the Yukon toward Dawson, another 2,000 miles away. By now the season was far advanced and the full blast of the northern winter had caught up with the stern-wheeler at Fort Yukon, north of the Arctic Circle. On October 2, 1898, the Captain found a blind slough where he put his boat in winter quarters. The following day he stepped over the steamer's low side and walked ashore on solid ice.

After the ice broke up that summer, the *Victorian* joined the Yukon River fleet. Lewis went on to other boats and new adventures in the fabulous North of the Gold Rush days, but after the passage of more than half a century he said that his clearest memory was the rescue of the *Victorian,* the boat that refused to stay wrecked. No wonder the memory has remained vivid! Probably not another vessel in Northwest maritime history has been rescued from a more hopeless or spectacular wreck. Captain Lewis and the *Victorian* proved that real seamanship is not confined to deep-sea ships.[1]

1.—The story of the *Victorian* first appeared in *Ships and Sailing,* February 1952, as part of an article by this author, titled "Stern-Wheelers North." It is reproduced by permission of the magazine's publishers, Kalmbach Publishing Company, Milwaukee, Wisconsin.

THE ALASKA GOLD RUSH

was going full blast by February of 1898. Glittering treasure of the Klondike had brought prosperity to the depression-ridden Pacific Northwest and business was booming. It had also brought a return to life for the worn-out hulks that for years past had rested drearily on mudflats and river backwaters. Scores of ancient steamers and windjammers were patched up, repainted, and sent north to garner part of the golden harvest. Some of them staggered wearily up the western seaboard from California and Oregon ports in the hope of striking it rich in their old age.

Such was the steam schooner *Clara Nevada,* out of Portland, Oregon. She had given the best years of her life to the United States Coast and Geodetic Survey as the *U. S.*

55

S. Hassler. Finally condemned and sold out of government service, the little iron steamer wound up carrying
passengers and freight to Alaska under her new name.
She left Dyea [1] on the black, stormy night of February 5,
1898, headed south. After that no one is quite sure what
happened to her. Watchers at Berner's Bay, south of
Dyea, saw the lights of a south-bound steamer suddenly
blotted out in a great ball of orange fire, but their small
boats could not buck the storm-lashed seas of the canal
to investigate the mysterious catastrophe. The *Clara
Nevada* never made port, so it was assumed that the suddenly extinguished ship had been the old steam schooner.

Later more definite evidence was found, though still
not much. Near the scene of her disappearance, fishermen
picked up her charred name board. Then the steamer
Rustler, out from Juneau, hauled in the burned body of
the lost steamer's purser. That just about settled it. The
Clara Nevada was gone and so were the twenty-eight men
of her crew. No one knew just how many passengers had
been aboard, for in gold rush days they never bothered
with pursers' lists. Informed guesses set the number at
about sixty-five. They were all gone too.

It was known that five important men from the gold
diggings were with the *Clara Nevada* on her mysterious
last voyage. These once-poor miners had piled up sudden
glittering fortunes in the first great, unbelievable Klondike cleanup; such men had caused the fabulous gold
rush. It was no wonder they boarded the first steamer to
the Outside when they reached Skagway, but it was ironic
for that steamer to have been the *Clara Nevada*. When
they boarded her, the five miners who had suddenly
struck it rich had no way of knowing that they were re-

1.—Dyea, a few miles across the flats from Skagway, was at that time a
boom town of ten thousand gold seekers and five thousand mules. In June,
1898, the Dyea baseball team, "the champions of the Far North," challenged
Soapy Smith's men of the Skagway Club to an all-out baseball battle. Today
Dyea is a ghost town, with a square mile of houses and business buildings,
but only one inhabitant.

turning all their hard-won gold to the rocky depths of
the North.

The pokes of dust and nuggets were locked in the
ship's strong-box. After the explosion and brief flames in
the night, the treasure also was gone. No other bodies
were found and no other wreckage, but there could be little doubt as to the fate of both ship and men. Records at
the Juneau Customs House report the following: "1898,
Feb. 5, Amer. Str. *Clara Nevada,* Lynn Canal, fire & explosion, total loss."

The small steam schooner did not have the page in the
Customs House records to herself. She was joined by
many other tired old ships before that year was over: the
schooners *Elsie, Sitka, Alexandria, Louise J. Kennedy,*
and *St. Lawrence;* the steamers *Whitelaw, Alfred J.
Beach, Mono, Marquis of Dufferin, Stickine Chief, Eliza
Anderson, Anita,* and *Brixham;* the ship *Sterling;* and
the bark *Guardian.*

There were plenty of ships to fill the disaster annals in
the gold rush year of 1898. The *Clara Nevada* was only
one of many and she was quickly forgotten despite the
strange, spectacular manner of her death and the large
number of men who died with her. Far more men had
died in the snow-choked passes ashore. Life was cheap
in Alaska that year. Soon the *Nevada* became just another
statistic in the Customs Record book at Juneau.

The lighthouse keeper at Elder Rock, Lynn Canal,
may never have heard of the *Clara Nevada* when he
watched a black storm come rushing down the narrow
waters one evening in 1908. It was a full decade, almost
to the day, from the stormy night of the old steamer's sudden end. In the ten years since then, Alaska had seen a
number of changes. Many of the familiar faces were gone.
The gold rush was a memory. At Elder Rock the lightkeeper may have been one of the newcomers, a *cheechako,*
but if he was an old-timer he may have thought briefly
of the strange fate of the *Clara Nevada* and of the miners

and the gold she carried. It was on just such a night that she met her doom.

Pitiless wind from the snow peaks was hurling itself down the canal. Great rollers were sweeping along before it to dash themselves high against the shuddering lighthouse tower. It was a night for the ghosts of ancient, long-dead ships to ride the dark waters of Lynn Canal. Through the slow, northern night the storm howled on. A high neap tide was pushed even higher by the storm waves surging down from the North. Great boulders rolled uneasily far below in the sea bed and, above the shouting of the storm, the lightkeeper in the tower could hear and feel the shifting of his small island's foundations.

Things looked better in the morning. At first they did. The tide had fallen. The lighthouse no longer seemed threatened by the sea's violence. The water had already retreated. The wind soon followed suit. Then the keeper emerged from his narrow fortress to inspect the tiny, rocky island that was his home. He felt sure that strange things had taken place during the night, but he was hardly prepared for what he found. Nothing much happened at the south end of the rock; the northern tip had received the brunt of the storm. He headed that way along the reef side of the island.

It was there that he found the long-lost steamer *Clara Nevada*—the steamer and all her people. The terrific wind and sea, coupled with the extreme high tide, had uncovered the ship's deep-hidden grave. The storm had carried the dead ship south to the point of Elder Rock. There it had flung its ghastly plaything ashore. It was probably fortunate for the lightkeeper that he did not see the *Clara Nevada* coming. What he had on his beach was unpleasant enough, but to have watched her approach might have been a bit too much for a lonely man on a little rock in the sea. What a sight it must have been, that pallid ship-corpse, dead and buried a full decade, coming in out of the night and the storm to spill its

skeleton crew ashore under the blindly-staring white eye
of the beacon light.

The five sourdoughs who helped launch the Alaska
Gold Rush were probably aboard for that strange, delayed landfall, but there was no way of telling the rich
from the poor, the lucky from the unlucky, aboard that
ship. Ten years in the rocky catacombs of the sea bottom
had robbed them of individuality along with life and
pokes of gold. From the wreck of the *Clara Nevada,*
many faces grinned at the lightkeeper but they all looked
dismayingly alike.

Yet people were no longer interested in how the steamer and her passengers had met their fate; they were concerned only with the gold she had carried. The sea,
though, had kept the treasure and cast up only bones.
Its answer to the *Nevada* mystery was most unsatisfactory,
for the strange resurrection only deepened that far greater enigma—the ways of the sea itself.

THE LITTLE ALASKA STEAMER

Clara Nevada was not the only mystery ship to return to the land of the living after vanishing for many years. The old iron steamship *Centennial* was gone almost as long—seven years—and though she carried no skeleton crew on her return, she was ghostly enough in her own right, being wrapped from truck to waterline in a white pall of ice.

Built in London in 1859, and originally called the *Delta*, she served under many flags and several names. The Japanese had her a while as the *Takasago Maru;* then the Alaska Steamship Company took her over for the northern run until she was sold to the Charles Nelson Company. As the *Centennial*, she was purchased from Nelson by Captain Kane of Seattle, subject to her safe arrival at Puget Sound from Japan, where she was then docked.

In 1906 she started out from Muroran for San Francisco carrying a cargo of sulphur, which was to be discharged in California before she sailed to Puget Sound.
She never made port. The usual routine for missing ships
was followed. Her name was placed on the overdue-ships'
list and her reinsurance rates went up. Lloyds finally
wrote her off their books. When no trace of the ship was
found in the next few years, it was assumed that the sulphur cargo had caught fire in mid-ocean, destroying ship,
cargo and crew. Insurance claims were paid and, with
the passing of the years, the old steamer *Centennial* was
forgotten.

Then, seven years after she had sailed, her ghost was
sighted. In 1913, a Russian exploring expedition was
steaming through the lonely reaches of the Okhotsk Sea,
off the Siberian Coast. As the ships skirted the leeward
side of Sakhalin Island, a lookout spotted the silhouette
of a long, slim steamer farther in toward the island. Seen
through the drifting mist, the strange ship was an eerie
spectacle. Pure white against the dark bulk of the lonely
island, she was solidly frozen in the offshore ice. Every
inch of her hull, masts and funnel was so thickly coated
with ice that she looked like some fantastic iceberg, carved
by nature in a ship's outline.

With true Russian stoicism, the fleet sailed on, leaving
the frozen ship in the cold embrace of Siberian ice.
Months later in the Orient the British pilot of the Russian
expedition met some American merchant marine officers
whom he told of the strange vision he had seen through
the misty veils of the Okhotsk Sea. He even described the
mysterious ship in considerable detail.

She was a steamer of unusual lines, flush decked, re-
markably long and slim, built more on the pattern of a
clipper ship than of the later iron cargo tanks. She had a
raking, clipper bow and an uncommon stern design. One
of the American officers had often visited aboard the *Centennial* and knew her well. He was also familiar with her

vanishing act seven years earlier. He was startled to
realize that the pilot was describing, in exact detail, the
old *Centennial*.

Later the facts were reconstructed this way: the ship
would normally have followed a course laid out to take
advantage of the eastward set of the Japanese Current.
This would have brought her within a hundred miles of
the Kuril Islands, the seaward guardians of the Okhotsk
Sea. A storm probably sent her clawing to leeward of the
islands for shelter. There she was caught in the ice. Her
captain was thought to have had aboard one of the old
British "blue maps" of that area. These maps indicated
a trading post on the mainland opposite Sakhalin Island
where the ship was frozen in. Chances are that the crew
deserted her, rowing and pulling the boats through
broken water and over ice floes to the mainland and the
safety of the trading post.

But there was no post. Long deserted, it had fallen
into ruins. The men of the *Centennial* would have found
no sanctuary there. They probably perished, one by one,
of cold and starvation in that uninhabited northern
wasteland. No survivors were ever seen. Only that single,
brief, dreamlike glimpse of the ship in her icy shroud
revealed the story of their fate.

That same year saw the solution of another old mystery of the sea, the loss of the British square-rigged Cape
Horn ship, *Marlborough* of Glasgow. She had left Lyttleton, New Zealand, in January, 1890, with a cargo of wool
and frozen mutton for the Clyde. She was commanded
by Captain Hird and carried a crew of thirty-three. Some
time later she was spoken at sea off Magellan. This was
the last that was heard from her and, in April, she was
posted at Lloyds as missing. A government cruiser made
a voyage to the coast of Patagonia in search of her but
found not so much as a splinter of wreckage. It was assumed that she had foundered somewhere off the Horn.
Ashore, a few widows went into mourning, as did the

Marlborough's underwriters, but in the course of the next twenty-four years she was forgotten, becoming just another Cape Horner that had lost her fight with the sea on the most desolate corner of the world.

Then, in December, 1913, another square-rigger came around Cape Horn road to Lyttleton with a story to tell of the ship *Marlborough,* gone from all human ken for almost a quarter of a century. Here it is, in the Captain's own words:

"We were off the rocky sea caves near Punta Arenas, keeping near the land for shelter. The caves are deep and silent, the sailing difficult and dangerous. It was a weirdly wild evening with the red orb of the sun setting on the horizon. The stillness was uncanny. From the jagged rocks to our right, a shining green light was reflected.

"We rounded a point into a deep-cleft cove. Before us, a mile or more across the water, stood a sailing vessel, with the barest shreds of canvas fluttering in the breeze. We signaled and hove to. No answer came. We searched the stranger with our glasses. Not a soul could we see, not a movement of any sort. Masts and yards were picked out in green, the green of decay.

"The vessel lay as if in a cradle. It recalled the *Frozen Pirate,* a novel that I read years ago. I conjured up the vessel of the story with her rakish masts and the 'outline of her six small brass cannon traced with snow.'

"At last we came up. Still there was no sign of life aboard. After a few minutes our first mate, with a member of the crew, boarded her. They met a startling sight. Below the warped wheel lay the skeleton of a man. Treading warily on the rotting deck, which cracked and broke where they walked, they encountered three skeletons in the hatchway. In the mess room were the remains of ten bodies, and on the bridge six more; one, possibly that of the captain. An uncanny stillness prevailed and the dank smell of mold made the flesh creep. We discovered a few remnants of books and a rusty cutlass in the captain's cabin. Nothing stranger in the history of the sea can ever have been seen. The first mate examined the still faint letters on the bows and with some effort read, '*Marlborough,* Glasgow.' "

Such sea mysteries would probably be considered far-fetched if they appeared in a book of fiction. It is difficult in today's radio-girt world to imagine such spectral ships lying unseen for a decade or a quarter of a century. But in the days when ships at sea lost all ties with the land as they sailed the vast, uninhabited waters of the globe, such things did happen. They help explain why the old-time windship sailormen were frankly and unashamedly superstitious. Sometimes they saw things that landsmen never see, like the death ship *Marlborough* in the silent, glimmering sea caves off Cape Horn.

IN THE GOOD OLD DAYS

before the turn of the century, the people of the Northwest Coast had a theory that their natural resources were boundless. Thousands of square miles of virgin timber stood between salt water and snow-crowned mountains. Settlers fought the forest to gain an acre or two for planting, and the sawmills on tidewater that shrieked away night and day only nibbled at the edges of the vast wilderness of fir and spruce and cedar. Timber of the Northwest Coast, it was believed, would last forever.

Thousands of ice-cold, clear-water streams boiled down in crystal purity from the mountains to the sea, and from the sea the salmon 'came to spawn and die in the fresh water where they were born. Some say that when the big salmon migrations were on, a man could cross many of the streams without touching the water, by simply walk-

65

ing on a moving carpet of great, silver fish. There was no thought of conservation. There was too much of everything, really more than could ever be used. At least people seemed to think so.

But Progress came to the Northwest Coast, riding the Northern Pacific parlor cars. Timber barons and fish kings and mining monarchs came, and they brought machinery and engines and dredges to reap the boundless harvest of the new frontier. Then forests fell back from the sea, leaving torn, ruined wastelands marked with the fire-blackened stumps of dead giants. Donkey engines yelled and spat sparks in tinder-dry summer forests and no one cared much when an empire of timber went up in smoke. There were more empires for the taking!

When cities began to pollute mountain streams and the clear, salt-water harbors, the silver fish refused to enter these waters. Then great fish traps and the purse seines replaced the fish spear and the dugout canoe. Finally the people of the Northwest Coast came to realize that their wealth was not boundless; that greed and the machine were fast stripping them of their heritage. Now they are feverishly building sewage disposal plants and tree nurseries and fish hatcheries, trying to restock the crops so ruthlessly destroyed for seventy years.

Both fish traps and the purse seines are gone from the inland sea now, but at the start of this century they were in operation on almost every bay and inlet. The steep, lonely shores of Whidbey Island were bordered thick with trap pilings, as were the green and lovely San Juans. Above the high-tide mark, the tents of the fishermen rose like mushroom cities, and the waters were alive with the small boats of trapmen, fish-buyers' tugs and barges, and the sturdy little ships of the seiners. In those days the islands of Puget Sound were teeming canvas cities, spilling over onto tidewater with uneven streets of bobbing boats, house barges, and floating stores and warehouses.

Upon this scene of prosperous activity there came, one fateful day, a gentleman of Levantine extraction and remarkable business acumen. It seemed to him that there was something missing from the fish empire of the islands and, being a purveyor of food and liquid refreshment and varied forms of entertainment, he was not long in deciding what this was. Here were thousands of men living solitary lives, blessed with heavy purses and virile health, yet with no place to spend either their physical or monetary wealth. They had no wine, no women, and so, of course, very little song. The Levantine gentleman, a true humanitarian, felt called upon to right this sorry state of affairs.

He departed for the civilian ports of the mainland where he negotiated the purchase of a large and commodious houseboat, a great barn of a building that floated buoyantly on a raft of cedar logs. He tastefully embellished its interior in the decor of the gay nineties, put up partitions to provide the snug privacy of hotel bedrooms, and added an imposing bar with a hogshead of high-voltage whiskey. Next, the new proprietor set about recruiting a crew for his staunch craft, which we shall, for the purpose of this otherwise factual narrative, call the *Idle Hour.* Lured by optimistic tales of the golden harvest to be reaped by the *Idle Hour,* the loveliest and most adventurous of the waterfront damsels flocked from the shoreside bistros and dance halls of Seattle and Port Townsend to this floating haven of joy. Then a tug was summoned and the boat moved majestically north, toward the shore of Whidbey Island.

The master and proprietor of this weird and wonderful vessel selected a convenient location just offshore from the point and moored his ship to a few decayed pilings from an abandoned trap. Shortly thereafter the amazing news spread along the length and breadth of Whidbey and across to the San Juans. The fishing empire was now blessed with a gentlemen's resort. Not only was good

liquor available—far different from the horrid panther-
juice served free on the fish-buyers' boats—but the fairest
damsels of skid road were there to provide companionship
and understanding to lonely and prosperous fishermen, at
a reasonable price, of course. Furthermore, the gala
opening was set for that very night.

The Levantine gentleman's highest hopes were realized. The debut of the *Idle Hour* was a tremendous success. Although the water was calm, the ark rocked and
swayed at its moorings. The piano banged bravely against
the uproar of talk and singing and bawdy jokes. A golden
harvest poured across the bar and back came a river of
amber whiskey for parched gullets. The girls, bright in
their shore-side finery, were ogled, fought over, and
swung dizzily around the tiny dance floor by a swarming
regiment of fishermen. As the evening wore on, the girls
felt things were getting a little rough but they all kept
stuffing the steady stream of goldpieces into their bod-
ices; the harvest of greenbacks into their silk stocking-
tops.

Such was the scene aboard the *Idle Hour* when the
crew of a Port Townsend cannery tug boarded her jumping decks with words of warning.

"Better let us pull you into the cove," they counseled.
"The barometer's dropping and the storm warnings are
up at Point Wilson. It'll be blowing a hell of a nor'wester
before morning."

As might have been expected, this sober advice was
drowned in the joyful tumult. Shaking their heads sadly,
the crew departed to tow a barge of salmon across the
straits. In the dark, early-morning hours, when revelry
was at its height aboard the *Idle Hour,* disaster struck.
The predicted northwest gale came whooping and screeching up the Straits of Juan de Fuca with all the power of
65,000,000 square miles of open sea behind it. The first
big swell sent whiskey glasses crashing and girls screaming. The second stood the *Idle Hour* on her head and

pulled the rotten piling from the sand. Those that followed hurled the ark on the beach and proceeded to
knock it into small pieces. From the wrecked and crumbling boat crawled and leaped and swam a mass of in-
ebriated fishermen, half-drowned bar tenders, and yelling
women. True to the traditions of the sea, the skipper of
the wrecked vessel was the last to leave, and he salvaged
all he could. Two unbroken barrels of whiskey he rolled
up the beach and, safe above high tide, sat down on one
of them, gazing wordless at the end of all his great dreams.

Day broke upon a desolate scene. A few drunken victims of the storm sprawled upon the beach, snoring
raucously. The Levantine gentleman kept his sad and
lonely vigil upon the cask of whiskey, but most of the
Idle Hour's survivors, including the bedraggled beauties
of the crew, had departed from that melancholy shore.
All that remained of the houseboat that had been so
proud and bright a few hours before were the great cedar
logs on the beach. That morning the shore of Whidbey
Island was a strange sight, lined with flotsam and jetsam
such as had never before been cast there in the memory
of man.

Mingled with the usual driftwood and fish heads along
the high-tide line were plumed bonnets and lace-edged
corsets, brass cuspidors and smashed whiskey glasses. A
kelp-draped oil painting of a voluptuous, unclothed
nymph lay propped against a ruined piano. A sobered,
departing fisherman averted his eyes as he stumbled over
an empty beer keg wearing a pair of frilled, silken
drawers.

One would think that outrageous fortune had loosed
a full quiver of slings and arrows upon the public-spirited
man who had sought to bring joy to the lonely fishermen
but, like a topmast in a typhoon, more disaster lay ahead.
Up steamed the U. S. Revenue Cutter *Grant* as fast as her
leaky boiler and asthmatic engine could drive her. Off
the point she dropped anchor and sent a boat in toward

shore. An officer of the Revenue Service approached the brooding Levantine gentleman.

"You are too late to do us any good," said that unhappy man. "The disaster, she has already occurred. You are always too late, and I am a ruined man."

"On the contrary," replied the officer, "we are not too late. Our primary duty is the enforcement of the revenue laws of the United States. I observe that you are seated upon a keg of whiskey and have another near by. Since this is more whiskey than you could possibly consume yourself, I assume that it is for sale. Kindly produce your license."

The Levantine gentleman had no license. He had intended to dispense this whiskey, not from the land but from the water where no license was required. Nevertheless, the whiskey was on land now and he was guilty of flagrant violation of the law of the Federal Government. Pitiful as it is to relate, he was dragged away, kicking and protesting, to the *Grant's* brig, to answer charges of possessing unlicensed whiskey.

The *Grant* was never a ship beloved by North Coast sailors. She interfered in too many neat and profitable smuggling deals and stayed too often at her dock, patching boilers or waiting for orders when sailormen needed her help. In 1907, the government sold her to the San Juan Fishing Company and four years later she was stranded off Banks Island, with 30,000 pounds of halibut in her holds. The crew escaped, but when the old *Grant* fell apart on the rocks, few mariners had a tear to spare for the ex-revenue cutter. They felt that an ironic justice had caught up with her. If our Levantine friend of the *Idle Hour* survived his many misfortunes, we can assume that he felt diabolic joy at news of the violent end of the U. S. Revenue Cutter *Grant*.

THOUGH THE CANADIAN freighter *Alpha* could not be classed as an unlucky ship, inasmuch as she had butted her way around the Pacific Ocean for thirty years, her crewmen declared that luck alone had kept her afloat during the last ten of these. A little old thousand-tonner built at Halifax in 1870, she was never a sea queen, and, by 1900, was downright disreputable. That was the year she made her last voyage and the year her luck ran out.

Owners of a steamship that has passed her thirtieth birthday have their problems. Crews hesitate to trust themselves to the rusty plates and loose rivets and underwriters are equally reluctant to hazard their funds by insuring an aging sister of the sea. The Canadian firm of Barber and Jansen had bought the *Alpha* in 1897 and diverted her from the Vancouver-West Indies run to the

71

Alaska route. They got her for $27,000 and, with the Klondike Gold Rush, were repaid several times over; but the easy pickings of the gold rush days were past, and the *Alpha* was fast becoming a headache instead of an asset.

When a fish-packing firm indicated that they would be willing to consign a cargo of salted dog salmon to the *Alpha's* rusty insides for transit to Japan, her owners saw a chance to kill two birds with one stone. The salmon cargo would pay the freighter's way to the Orient, then they would sell her in China, which was the last billet of many worn-out steamers. On paper this looked good, but the *Alpha's* luck had run out.

A small army of nautical gentlemen boarded her at her Vancouver dock, looked around, and departed shoreward as rapidly as possible. Even after gaining the shore, many of them kept glancing backward apprehensively as if they expected the steamer to sink from sight below the wharf she was leaning against. No captain could be found who was so hard up as to covet a place on the *Alpha's* rickety bridge; no engineer could be discovered who was drunk or crazy enough to trust himself anywhere within the range of her boilers; and no deckhands were willing to sling their sea bags in her dank and leaky fo'c'sle. In short, not a seaman in Vancouver would ship aboard the S. S. *Alpha*.

Finally, in desperation the owners imported from distant places a crew of men who had never seen or heard of the ship. These were sent aboard in the dead of night when kindly darkness masked the old tub's manifold blemishes. Their orders were to start for Japan the first thing in the morning. In the gray, December dawn the Vancouver waterfront was awakened by the weird farewell af the *Alpha's* whistle. She blubbered steam, burped, moaned sadly, then subsided in a tremulous falsetto. The lines came in and the steamer veered reluctantly away from the dock that had supported her for so long, thrusting her blunt snout down Burrard Inlet. As she headed

for the Orient where they would see her no more, her
owners were happy men.

But, alas for the hopes of steamship owners, she got no
farther than Victoria. Her crew brought her in very low
in the water with the pumps working hard. They announced that she had sprung a leak. Then, to a man, they
deserted her; and, except for the chief engineer, none of
them was ever seen again. Before leaving town he
paused for a drink or two and the enraged owners had
him jailed for desertion. Happily relaxed in the Victoria
jail, he announced that this was paradise compared to
the engine room of the S. S. *Alpha* and that he would
rather stay in jail for life than go back aboard that maritime swill-bucket.

The *Alpha's* owners now faced the whole problem
again; only this time it was complicated by the fact that
the ship was half full of water and her ill-fame had
spread even farther abroad. When they had her pumped
out and found that she leaked no worse than usual, their
suspicions were confirmed that the crew had opened her
seacocks. They became even more determined to get her
to the Far East, where they could unload her on some
unsuspecting Chinese. Next time, the managing owner,
Samuel Barber, was to go along to encourage the crew
and guard against dirty work.

With another crew somehow enticed aboard, the
Alpha once more girded her rusty loins for the voyage
across the Pacific. She sailed on December 16, 1900. The
short winter day fled westward ahead of her and a very
black December night came up astern. At 10 p. m. she
was still waddling through the Strait of Georgia when a
howling gale swept down from the north to send her
staggering. Never quick to answer her helm, the old
freighter steered like a steam roller under the gale's
buffeting.

Through the spray and driven sleet, her master, Captain Yorke, could see the great winking eye of Yellow

Island Light. He knew that he must soon take the wallowing, yawing freighter through the 400-foot channel between the light and the black bulk of Vancouver Island. With two quartermasters fighting the groaning wheel, the old steamer swung her rust-streaked bows toward the channel. But as wind and sea took over, she lurched on around drunkenly, headed for the offshore rocks. There was just one thing for the Captain to do. He put her about in a full circle to try for the even narrower channel on the seaward side of Yellow Island. Only 250 feet of deep water separated the stone ledge supporting the lighthouse from the jetting reefs to seaward. That was not enough sea room for the *Alpha*. As if determined upon suicide, the tired steamer plunged and bucked and fought her helm, at last succeeding in getting her own head.

Then she piled up on the rock ledge at the foot of the lighthouse tower. Great seas rolled in, exploded against her battered hull, and swept shoreward carrying lifeboats, hatch covers, and parts of her superstructure. Engineers Matterson, Murray, and Dunn stayed down in the flooded, steam-filled inferno of the engine room where they worked the pumps and generator until the last. They kept the wheel turning too, so the *Alpha* had to keep her bows pressed hard on the ledge. Captain Yorke and owner Barber stayed on the bridge.

The devotion to duty of these brave men saved most of the crew. From their end, the lighthouse men helped, somehow stretching a lifeline between the broken ship and the lighthouse. Then, one by one, twenty-five men were drawn to safety in the tower, before the line broke. Water flooded the engine room; the fires were out. The engineers had died at their posts and the ship was dead too. Without power, she swung broadside to wind and sea and began to fall apart in huge chunks. Three hours from the time she struck, the *Alpha* was gone. Not a trace of her remained above the water.

Nine men, including one of her owners, her Captain and her engineers, went down with the *Alpha* off Yellow Island Light. It seemed that the ocean had done its worst, but more of the ill-fortune that dogged the old ship on her last voyage was to follow. The surviving partner was supposed to get insurance on her cargo before she sailed. Having planned a week-end trip to Seattle, he had put the business off until Monday. On Monday the insurance agent was home with a cold. The upshot of all the delay ashore was the loss at sea of an uninsured cargo.

Thirty years of bad luck had caught up with the Canadian freighter *Alpha,* and the voyage that was to dispose of her at a tidy profit killed one of her owners and left the other with a crushing load of debt. That, if nothing else, makes the story of the *Alpha* an unusual one, for generally only simple seamen are the victims of a ship's bad luck and an owner's urge for profit.

OF ALASKA'S INSIDE PASSAGE
scenic attractions, Taku Inlet, a few miles south of
Juneau, is one of the most widely advertised. On the run
down narrow Lynn Canal from Skagway to Juneau,
southbound steamship passengers are treated to a wealth
of scenic grandeur, but the most spectacular exhibit comes
last. The massive bulk of Douglas Island looming up to
mark the end of Lynn Canal is the sentinel of Taku Inlet. Almost abreast of the island's southern tip the inlet
slices northeast by southwest into the Alaska mainland.

At its head are the twin glaciers of Foster and Windom.
Foster Glacier is "dead." Its age-old movement to the
sea has stopped and it spawns no icebergs. Windom
Glacier is very much alive. A vast, gently-sloping mountain of ice, it climbs five thousand feet above the sea, its
foot a sheer ice wall towering perpendicularly above the
76

biggest steamer's mastheads. Excursion liners always pause off Taku to blow their whistles. Sometimes the blast is all that is needed to coax the great ice mountain into its sensational act. A frozen mass as tall as a city sky-scraper slowly detaches itself from the parent glacier, top-ples majestically on the brink, then makes its awesome plunge into the sea, culminating a drama that has been thousands of years in the making.

But bergs do not always wait for a steamer's whistle. They were dropping from the face of Taku a thousand years before James Watt invented the steam engine and it is quite likely that they will be dropping a thousand years from now, steam whistles or not. Taku Inlet is often peopled with the children of the glacier. A ghostly, white fleet, the great bergs drift, sometimes huddling and grind-ing together on the tide's flood at the foot of the ice cliffs; sometimes venturing out, on the ebb, past the portals of the inlet to add an overtone of pallid menace to the already manifold perils of the Inland Passage.

So it was that a great berg coursed into the sea from Windom Glacier in the summer of 1901. For a while it ghosted aimlessly about the inlet, drifting outward with the tide, then circling backward to muzzle ponderously against the mother glacier. It melted a little during its meandering, water that had congealed in the glacial age mingling with the salt sea water of the Inland Passage. But, on the evening it left home for good, it was still as big and as tall as a square block of downtown Manhattan. It was near mid-August and the runoff of melted snow and ice added to the offshore set of the tide. An offshore breeze sprang up to help the mighty berg along as it traveled in company with countless other floating ice mountains, many smaller, a few even vaster than itself. By midnight of August 4, 1901, it had drifted out toward the center of Stephens Passage, a few miles south of Juneau.

Two hours later the great berg and its companions of the ghostly fleet were invisible. A dense fog bank had

been wafted down the glacier inlet on the last breath of
the offshore breeze and lay right across Stephens Passage,
blotting out ice and water and sky. It was a narrow fog
bank, only a mile or so across. Clear, black water and
starry, night sky extended both north and south of it.
Only the playground of the glacier's children was hidden
by the white cloak of mist. Northward toward Juneau,
the water was brightened by the reflected lights of a fast-
moving steamship.

The S. S. *Islander,* flagship of the Canadian Pacific
Navigation Company fleet and pride of the northern
water routes, was headed Outside. She was steaming fast,
as always, piling up a great, gleaming mound of phos-
phorescent water under her slim prow and sending the
liquid fire of her bow wave in a spreading fan of light
across the dark waterway. The black smoke rolled from
her two smartly-raked buff funnels while, under deep,
quiet water, the quick beat of her twin screws reverber-
ated in muffled thunder.

The *Islander* was not a new ship. She had been built
in Scotland thirteen years earlier, especially for the Canadian Pacific's northern service. But she was still un-
surpassed in speed and beauty. She had inaugurated the
age of modern water transportation in the Pacific Northwest, and she would probably be a good-looking ship if
she were afloat today. Her fine-lined steel hull was 240
feet long, with a 42-foot beam. Her smoothly powerful
triple-expansion engines and twin screws were capable of
driving her at twenty knots. During her thirteen years of
service in Canadian and Alaskan waters she had never
been in a serious scrape; rather, she had built up a great
reputation for speed and reliability. She was the "lucky
flagship" and people felt safe on her. Even if she should
strike a hidden rock or an iceberg she would be all right,
they said, for the *Islander* was practically unsinkable. Her
hull was divided into watertight compartments which,
in an emergency, could be sealed off at a moment's

notice.   Eleven years later, people were saying the same thing about another great steamship, the *Titanic*.

The *Islander* had left Skagway for Victoria on the evening of Wednesday, August 14, 1901, carrying one of her largest passenger lists since the height of the Alaska Gold Rush. Many of those who had boarded her at Skagway were sourdoughs from the White Horse River country, their backs bent with the weight of the sacked gold dust they carried aboard. Estimates of the value of the dust and nuggets stowed in the purser's safe ran as high as three million dollars. The ship's company consisted of seventy-seven first-class passengers, thirty second-class, five children too small to need tickets, three stowaways, five "workaways," and a crew of sixty-one, totaling 181.

It is a gala day at Skagway when any steamer leaves for Outside. The *Islander,* with her huge fortune in gold, was a very special steamer. The lucky miners, going out to spend their hard-earned wealth, put on a dress rehearsal of the contemplated celebration ahead. Most of them came aboard carrying a full head of steam and they kept their boilers stoked at the steamer's well-stocked bar. The drinks were on the miners, who welcomed all comers, particularly the pilot, the fine fellow who would guide them safely to the bright lights of civilized seaports to the south. According to many subsequent accounts, the *Islander's* pilot joined the festivities at Skagway and felt no pain for the rest of the voyage.

As the steamer slashed her way from Juneau in the early minutes of Thursday, August 15, the bar and smoking room held a handful of late celebrants. A few passengers lingered on deck, watching the dark bulk of Douglas Island slip by to starboard. One of these, a veteran of many voyages on the *Islander,* counted the turns of the racing screws.

"One hundred and one- two- three- four. She's turning up 104 revolutions to the minute," he observed to a friend as he snapped closed the cover of his watch. "That means she's doing a good fifteen knots. Maybe seventeen if the tide's with us."

At that moment the *Islander* cut deep into the fog bank that hid the mouth of Taku Inlet.

In the saloon, Captain H. R. Foote, with a group of male passengers, was enjoying a post-midnight lunch. Earlier in the evening his temper had been a bit ragged. The pilot had left the bridge, weaving noticeably, and told him he would like to be excused from his watch for a little while. He was not feeling well.

"All right," said the Captain, "you go and lie down and I'll take care of her."

But he had already stood one watch on the bridge that evening and was tired. When the pilot reported back for duty, the Captain was glad to turn the watch over to him and get below to the warmth of the cabins. He was having a bite to eat and a last cup of coffee as the steamer became enveloped in the white mantle of the glacial fog.

Overhead the steam whistle shattered the night with its first warning blast, but the racing engine did not slow its beat. Again the siren bellowed out, its great voice sounding lonely and lost and a bit muffled in the full depths of the misty blanket that shrouded the ship.

Up in the bows the lookout sniffed the air. He could see nothing, but he could smell danger, the subtle, unmistakable scent of ice.

Steam sobbed and roared again from the whistle on the forward stack, and the echo returned to the ship with frightening suddenness. The sound had leaped back from something much nearer than the close-pressing shores of Douglas Island and the mainland. Hidden by the cold, sad fog of the very early morning, the mysterious sounding board was dead ahead. It was the mighty iceberg, calved by Taku's glacier and wandering on the crest of the summer tide.

No time remained for another questioning blast from

the ship. Squarely and stunningly, the *Islander* struck the massive ice mountain. The shock awakened most of the passengers and crew, who were asleep below, but many of them were no better off awake than asleep. The steamer's hull had buckled, jamming their stateroom doors tight shut.

After that things happened fast—a frenzied nightmare in double time. Dashing to the bridge, Captain Foote was met by the pilot who reported that the ship had struck an iceberg. Watertight doors were closed and passengers who had been able to get out of their rooms were told there was no danger. Some of them, remembering that the *Islander* was unsinkable, went back to bed, ashamed of their momentary panic.

Then the chief engineer reported that water was pouring in below far faster than the pumps could handle it. When it was finally realized that the unsinkable *Islander* had received a mortal blow, chief steward Simpson, with other ship's officers, formed a rescue party. Armed with fire axes, they smashed in doors and passageways, freeing passengers and clearing obstructions from the escape routes. The thundering blows of the axes told their own story of desperation; and, in wild confusion, frightened passengers poured onto the decks.

Boats were lowered but few were filled to capacity. One, designed to hold more than forty persons, drifted off into the fog with just seven in it. The third boat away from the sinking liner carried only seventeen. Passengers milling on the deck were dazed with sleep and shock and panic.

The steamer was going down fast, sinking by the bow. The stern rose from the water, the screws still racing madly in foggy air. One of the drifting lifeboats barely escaped the crazy arc of the massive propeller on the ship's port side. As the hull sank lower in the water, it was racked by a great explosion. The whole house and upperworks appeared to rise from the decks. Then the lights went out and the *Islander* was gone.[1]

Some of the White Horse miners had secured their satchels of gold before the ship went down. In their extremity most of them abandoned the treasure to save their lives, but at least one of them was determined to take it with him, and he did. He plunged overboard clutching a suitcase full of gold, $40,000's worth. Neither the miner nor the gold ever came up from that plunge.

The unfilled boats drifted away from the wreck and were soon lost in the fog. Most of the ship's company were left floundering in the icy water or clinging to bits of wreckage. After an hour or two some of the boats, guided by the cries of those still alive, found their way back to the tragic scene, but many failed to survive a two-hour dip in the glacial waters. All told, forty-two lives and a fabulous hoard of gold were lost with the steamship *Islander*. The Captain was one of those who died.

"Tell them I tried to beach her," were his last words as he slipped from the torn ship's fragment that had supported him for a short time. Those who saw him go seemed to think that he made no effort to save himself.

At dawn, a volunteer party, led by chief engineer Brownlee and the mate, walked up the beach toward Juneau in search of help. They reached the Treadwell Mine, where the steamers *Flossie* and *Lucy* were at the dock with steam up. By noon the *Flossie* was at Juneau with her flag at halfmast, the *Islander's* survivors crowded on deck and six of the dead laid out below.

1.—It was reported at the time that the boilers had exploded as the ship sank. This is a controversial point, but most experts agree that the sudden inrush of cold water to the boilers of a sinking vessel cannot cause them to explode. One old-time engineer reports in the English magazine, *Sea Breezes,* "What really happens is that, as the ship sinks, water rushes into the furnaces and steam is generated in great volume, issuing with a violent roar from the funnel and any openings from the stokehold. The boilers do *not* burst. The noise is terrifying to the layman."

In such cases, probably a violent eruption of compressed air from the ship's hull does most of the damage, with the boilers providing ominous sound effects.

Fire has always been rated among the worst perils of the sea. It was especially to be feared in the days of wooden ships like the big Puget Sound steamer *Eastern Oregon*, reduced to a charred hulk by an 1891 conflagration.

The *Princess May* was rescued from this spectacular wreck, caused—some say—by the presence of a Jade Buddha.

The old bark *Coloma* during her last hours off the Graveyard.

Not until Sunday, August 18, when the steamer *Queen* arrived at Victoria, did word of the disaster reach the outside world. Early that evening, she nosed into Victoria's Outer Wharf, where a sizable crowd had gathered to welcome her. Hardly had she touched the dock when the purser shouted to some acquaintance in the crowd:

"The *Islander* has gone down with twenty-four passengers and sixteen of her crew!" The news spread like wildfire across the British Columbia capital and, in a matter of minutes, the city was in ferment. The disaster was, of course, magnified in the telling until many believed that the ship had been lost with all hands. Newspaper accounts of that date set the toll at from fifty-five to sixty.

It was three years before the hull of the *Islander* was discovered, lying in forty fathoms of water. Hopeful boatmen did much grappling for they had heard of the lost wealth in the sunken treasure ship, but they brought up only a few barnacle-encrusted steel plates. They disposed of these for nearly their weight in gold, as souvenirs of Alaska's worst marine tragedy. It was not until 1934, thirty-three years after the disaster, that improved salvage techniques raised the rusted hulk of the *Islander*. But her reported treasure was not aboard. Gold was found in the wreckage, yet it was only a hundredth part of what the legends of the ship had credited her with, and not enough to pay the costs of the salvage operations.

Some say the *Islander* never did carry the golden hoard that was attributed to her, that the miners carried their wealth in less romantic and less durable bank drafts. Some say the bulk of the treasure was in gold, but that it went overboard with the frightened passengers who tried to swim ashore but failed. Still others theorized that the treasure had been pirated in earlier grappling operations. No one is quite certain what the true story is. Until 1952 the rusted hulk of the *Islander* lay deserted on a quiet reach of the Inland Passage, a silent monument to another mystery of northern waterways. Then it was broken up and sold as scrap metal.

SOUTH FROM CAPE FLATTERY
to the mouth of the Quillayute River lies one of the wild-
est and most magnificent expanses of American coastline.
It is lonelier now than it was a century and a half ago
before white men came to the Pacific Northwest, for the
Indians who once dwelt there are dead and their villages
are long since gone. No human inhabitant, white or red,
is to be found on all the forty miles of coastline from the
Quillayute to Mukkaw Bay. No automobiles race honk-
ing up and down this beach, nor is it bordered with summer cottages. Hot-dog stands, curio shops and tourist
courts never interrupt its shoreline. It is a lonesome
beach and those who reach it must do so on foot.

The occasional hardy beachcomber who does pack in
over timbered trails is well rewarded. The beach is
strewn with the spoils of the Japan Current—the wreck-

84

age of ships, great glass floats from the nets of Oriental fishermen, and flotsam and jetsam of all the vast Pacific. There are reminders, too, of ships that met their doom on that grim, forsaken shore. Near Cape Johnson, almost hidden among tall ferns and creeping vines, lies a fallen concrete monument. Scrape away the mold and evergreen needles and you will find that it marks the final resting place of five men and one woman from the Chilean bark *Leonore,* who died on this abandoned northern coast.

It was midnight of October 3, 1893, and a raging gale with the screeching of a thousand harpies swept in across the immense void of the Pacific, whipping the deep-sea rollers in titanic spouting fury against the offshore rocks and jagged headlands. There, beyond the line of breakers, a sailing ship staggered, masts swaying against the dim horizon in a crazy death dance. Closer and closer to the white welter of the beach she swung, then lurched drunkenly as the deathblow struck and her tall masts went crashing down. Despairing cries drifted in on the gale, but then, as now, there was no one on that desolate shore to hear them. Dim lights were drowned out and exhausted men crawled from the welter of foam up the gently-sloping beach. Last of all, the dead came rolling in.

The *Leonore* was almost at the end of her long voyage from Iquique to Puget Sound when the 70-mile-an-hour blasts of that October gale caught up with her just south of Flattery. In the howling wilderness of crashing seas and blinding, wind-driven rain, the captain soon lost his bearings. Then a dark shape loomed up on the weather bow. The lookout reported it as another ship, but it was only one of the isolated pillar rocks guarding that coast. The helm was put down and a moment later the ship struck on the rocky shore. Losing his head completely, the captain jumped overboard with his wife clasped in his arms. A great sea dashed them back against the ship's side, killing them instantly.

On the deck all was confusion. Tremendous seas were breaking clear across the ship; the northwest hurricane was shrieking through the rigging, and the hull was grinding horribly on the rocks. Anything seemed better than waiting on that stricken ship; the cook, carpenter and one seaman followed the captain and his wife. Only the sailor reached shore alive.

Thirty minutes after she struck, the ship broke into pieces and the rest of the crew were driven ashore on bits of wreckage. The boatswain succumbed to the cold, slipped from the wreckage and was drowned. The rest of the men, barefoot and scantily clad, reached shore and made their way up the coast to Neah Bay. Next day a tug skirted the breaker line off Cape Johnson, but not a sign of the bark *Leonore* remained to mark her last resting place. Now, even the concrete pillar erected to mark the grave of those who died with her has fallen and, in a few more years, will be lost in the creeping underbrush of the dark, tidal forest.

A few miles farther north, near the mouth of the Ozette River, stands another memorial to victims of that dark, deserted shore. Cut in the stone are the names of eighteen men and boys and this inscription:

> "Here lies the crew of the bark *Prince Arthur* of Norway . . . foundered January 2, 1903."

The *Prince Arthur* was an iron bark of 1,600 tons, built at Birkenhead in 1869, as the British *Houghton Head*. She was en route from Valparaiso to British Columbia for a lumber cargo when she met her fate in much the same manner as the *Leonore*. This time a light in the shore window of a timber cutter's shack was the false beacon that lured a ship to her death. Thinking it was the beacon on Tatoosh Island, the captain steered toward it, stranding his ship on the rocky shore fifteen miles south of Tatoosh Light. She broke up almost immediately; still there was no panic or hysteria as there had been on the Chilean bark. Most of the crew were young apprentices, but they behaved like seamen. Captain Markusson saw one working at the boats without a life jacket. Removing his own, he handed it to the youngster, saying, "Take it, my lad. You need it worse than I."

Blue lights burned and rockets flared, yet there was no one to see them and bring help. In the face of that violent sea and heedless shore, all the bravery and devotion of the Norwegian seamen were useless. Only Hansen, the second mate, and Larsen, the sailmaker, reached shore alive.

Woodsmen and Indians cared for the two survivors and buried the eighteen dead crewmen in shallow graves above the beach. When the mail carrier brought word of the disaster to Seattle, by way of a 25-mile forest trail, a group of Norwegians made the long trip to the lonely beach. On a bluff overlooking the sea they cleared a plot and dug a grave for the young Norse sailors of the bark *Prince Arthur*. They wrapped the bodies in a great sail from their ship and placed a carved door from the ship as a marker. Later, Norwegian-Americans purchased the little plot of ground and erected there the tall stone shaft which still stands above that beautiful, menacing beach, a reminder of the scores of ships and seamen that have perished there: the German square-rigger *Flottbek,* the American bark *Nellie,* the steamer *Southerner,* the barks *Austria* and *Hattie Besse,* the steam schooner *Diana,* the ship *Commodore,* the schooner *Eliza,* and the barkentine *Free Trade.* The roll is long and melancholy, for almost every mile of this empty beach has seen some ship in her last agony.

Only the lonely graves above the booming surf and the half-buried wreckage in the sand remind the stray wanderer that, when the winter westerlies boom in from across the Pacific, this vast solitude is a grim lee shore under whose shifting sands lies buried a fleet of sailing ships.

UNTIL FAIRLY RECENTLY, SHIPPING
pages of the world's newspapers printed a regular feature
that is now happily deleted from maritime news. Usually
headed "Overdue Ships," it listed the merchant vessels,
almost always windships, that had sailed for some port or
other but had failed to arrive within a reasonable length
of time. Ships still go missing; they put out to sea and are
swallowed up without so much as a floating life buoy or
shattered lifeboat ever returning to shore. But such
tragedies are rare now, for this is an age of radio and of
far-sweeping rescue planes, always poised to respond to
the first electronic call for help. It is difficult today to vis-
ualize the complete isolation of a long-voyage windjammer of even thirty years ago.

Deep laden with lumber or coal, wheat or fish, those
ships dropped their tugs off Flattery; and, with a last

farewell from the towboat's steam whistle as canvas blossomed from the yards, their graceful hulls lay over to the push of the wind. Barks, square-rigged ships, and barkentine, all swept over the horizon.

Tatoosh Light would report them, outbound, to the cable stations ashore. Then they were alone on the Cape Horn road or the long haul to Australia or the Orient. Occasionally an inward-bound ship would pass them somewhere along the trackless ocean trade routes and report them on arrival. Frequently they made the whole voyage without sighting another ship, and, too often, they were never seen again in any port. After being listed for some time in the "Overdue Ships" column, they would receive some such direful attention as this:

"Nov. 26, 1916: Little hope remains for the safety of the well-known French bark *Marachel de Villars,* long overdue from Puget Sound to Ipswich with her grain cargo. The vessel is out 220 days, which would certainly seem to make her fully two months overdue. The *Marachel de Villars* left the Sound, April 21, and the next heard of her was when she was spoken, September 4, in latitude 47:37 north, longitude 14:07 west. From this position she should have reached her destination in three weeks or a month at most."

Usually that was the end of the story, for there really was no story. The ship, with all her crew, was gone. Again there was no answer to the ancient riddle of the sea. Once in a while, months or even years later, a floating bottle containing a hastily scrawled message would be found telling of the ship's fate. Sometimes in a faraway port would appear a lifeboat full of gaunt, bearded seamen to relate the death of their ship in remote waters. But, more often, these ships simply disappeared. The bell at Lloyds was tolled for them; the insurance was paid on ship and cargo—not on crewmen, who were expendable—; and ships and men were both soon forgotten.

The list of ships that sailed from the Northwest Coast

to a mysterious fate is far too long to record in full. The barks *Lord Raglan, W. C. Parke* and *Sierra Nevada;* the full-rigged ships *Brodich Castle, Grace Darling* and *Ivanhoe;* the brig *Hogdon;* the sloop *Cornelius;* the steamers *Montserrat, Keewenah, St. Denis* and *Estelle;* and the British clipper *Andrada* are only a few of that vanished fleet.

The *George S. Wright,* an American steamship, did not go missing in the true sense of the word inasmuch as bits of her wreckage were found on Alaskan beaches. Nevertheless her exact fate has remained a mystery for almost eighty years. Indian pirates, mutiny, a hidden reef, a boiler explosion—each of these has been suggested as the real reason this ship never made port.

In her day, the pride of Puget Sound and one of the first seagoing steamers built in the Pacific Northwest was the famous *George S. Wright.* She was launched at Port Ludlow in 1863, a 116-foot propeller steamship with auxiliary sails. For a while she ran between the Columbia River and British Columbia, then worked in Siberian waters for the Russian-American Telegraph Company; but, from 1869 until her final voyage, she carried the mails between Oregon, Puget Sound and Alaska.

In January, 1873, she sailed from Portland on her last trip. Arriving at Sitka, she discharged her northbound cargo to take aboard an assorted shipment of salmon, oil, hides, and furs for state-side ports. On her return voyage south she also took twelve passengers, mostly army people. The *Wright* put in at Tongass and at the fishing village of Kluvok. After that she was never seen again. For many days she was reported missing and the government was asked to send a revenue cutter to search for her. Until well into the twentieth century the Federal authorities moved very slowly in such matters. Before proceeding on rescue missions, cutter captains had to await orders from Washington. Often these were issued too late to do any good.

Such was the case with the *George S. Wright*. Weeks passed before a cutter was sent north. By that time the British Navy's *Petrel* and the merchant steamer *Gussie Telfair,* running mate to the lost steamer, had completed a thorough but fruitless search.

In those days the Northern Indians were still fierce and piratic. Since the steamer had Indian coal-passers and steward's helpers, it was suspected that these had contrived to put the ship out of commission off some lonely beach where their tribesmen could push out in canoes and make short work of both ship and ship's company. Another theory held that the steamer had struck an unmarked rock and foundered, with the shore-side Indians finishing off the survivors. Others believed that a boiler explosion had wiped out the ship with all hands.

Months later a portion of a human body clothed in an army uniform drifted ashore near Cape Caution; then the fully-clothed body of a small boy wearing a life-preserver. Pieces of wreckage came ashore at the same place. After a lapse of five years an Indian named Billy Coma announced that he was a survivor of the *George S. Wright*. According to him, the ship had struck a rock and foundered, and all the passengers and crew except himself and another Indian had been murdered by the natives. Though Billy Coma had never served aboard the *Wright* and was a notorious stranger to the truth, many of the details of his yarn were accurate. Probably his account was true except that he was in the native pirate band rather than in the crew of the lost ship. Anyhow, his is the only real clue to the fate of the steamship *George S. Wright,* gone missing in the Inland Passage these eighty years.

Year by year, the list of missing ships grew, the closing of 1894 adding three names in rapid succession — the steamers *Montserrat* and *Keweenah* and the square-rigged ship *Ivanhoe*. More than eighty men were lost in that trio of disasters. The stately *Ivanhoe* was towed out to sea by the tug *Tyee* and made sail in company with

the barkentine *Robert Sudden,* which had cast off from
her towboat at about the same time. The two windships
stayed close together until the next day, when a strong
southeasterly sprang up. This grew to full gale propor-
tions, bringing sheets of rain and hail that blotted out
both sea and sky. Blowing itself out in a few hours, the
storm revealed an ocean empty except for the barkentine.
The full-rigged ship had vanished utterly. The only
wreckage to come ashore from the square-rigger merely
added to the mystery surrounding her fate. On the shores
of Barclay Sound, Vancouver Island, a life buoy was
picked up with the name *Ivanhoe* stenciled on it. The
ship's name board was discovered embedded in the sand
at the entrance to Willapa Bay, 150 miles south of the
point where the buoy was found.

The best theory, based on the wreckage recovered, is
that the *Ivanhoe* raced south before the gale far faster
than the barkentine; that, near the mouth of the Columbia, some sea, greater than the rest, swept her deck and
smashed in her hatches; and that, heavily laden with a
cargo of coal, she sank like a rock, without warning.
Then the relentless northern drift picked up the two
bits of wreckage, the name board being carried ashore
by some fluke of wind and tide at Willapa, the life buoy
floating on up the coast to the Graveyard. At best, this is
only a theory. When ships go missing they leave no certain clues to their fate.

Early in December of that same year, 1894, two more
coal carriers joined the roster of missing ships. The
Montserrat and *Keweenah,* out from British Columbia
for California, left the Straits of Juan de Fuca at about
the same time, on the evening of December 7. They
were last seen, by the lookout at Tatoosh, about ten miles
out, plunging head on into an increasing southwest gale,
the *Montserrat* a little in the lead. As darkness shut
down, the watchers at the light station saw an immense
sea sweep in to blot both ships from sight. And that was

the last ever seen of either one. They simply vanished.

Captain David Blackburn, who owned and skippered the *Montserrat,* was a Nova Scotian seaman and a rip-roaring, swashbuckling shipmaster of the old — and not too ethical—school. He started out as a Columbia River fisherman but ended as a ship-owner and captain, known in all the West Coast ports as "Lucky Blackburn." He skippered many of the famous coastal liners—*Al Ki, Umatilla, Willamette* and *Walla Walla* — with never a breakdown, a stranding, or any of the manifold misfortunes that plagued most coastal skippers in those days. In fact, other seamen's misfortunes made Lucky Blackburn's fortune. He was always running across sinking or disabled ships and hauling them into port to collect juicy salvage checks.

He took the *Montserrat* to the Gilbert Islands on blackbirding expeditions, a trade closely akin to that of the old-time slave ships. There were whispers of smuggling escapades, but the skipper's luck held and he soon had a controlling interest in his ship. Placing her in the coal trade, he tested to the utmost his proverbial good luck. More cargo meant more profits and there was no Plimsoll mark on the *Montserrat's* side. If there had been, Captain Blackburn would have ignored it. His ship usually looked like a submarine with a funnel and yardarms when it left the straits.

Of course he had many hairbreadth escapes, but when crewmen, friends or steamboat inspectors timidly suggested more freeboard and less driving, the captain would just grin at them through his pirate's mustache and boom, "Never mind her. She's all right. She can climb a tree!"

Perhaps, with his overloaded collier, Lucky Blackburn tried to climb one too many trees. Perhaps she dipped into one last great sea and just never came up again. Maybe the *Keweenah,* less sturdy than the *Montserrat,* broke down, and Lucky Blackburn tried for another salvage fee. He had often put lines aboard other ships, hauling them to safety when most captains would have been hard pressed to save their own vessels. If he tried hauling in that wild December gale, the steamers might have rammed together and foundered. No one has ever been sure just how many persons went down with the *Montserrat*. Blackburn may have been a blackbirder, possibly a smuggler, but he was openhearted and generous. He seldom sailed his ship without a number of non-paying guests aboard who could not afford passage on the regular liners. When his famous luck ran out, his equally famous generosity brought anonymous death to those he tried to help. They perished along with the rest when the *Montserrat* went missing with the *Keweenah* off Flattery.

Sometimes tidings of disaster were found on the Graveyard before the ships involved even had time to be listed in the missing ships' column. This happened in the case of the square-riggers *Andrada* and *Ardnamurchan*. At the turn of the century, the close of the fishing season would bring a fleet of British salmon clippers to the Fraser River to load canned fish for Liverpool. Late in 1901, a number of them started the long voyage home. The *Clan Mackenzie* sailed in October; the *Fiery Cross* in November; the *Andrada* and *Ardnamurchan*, with a hold full at almost the same time, in December; the *Naiad*, a few days later, and the *Machrilianish*, December 29.

Early in January, grim wreckage began to come ashore on Vancouver Island's lee shore: cases of canned salmon, wooden dunnage, a pair of ten-foot oars branded with the letter "A," and finally a teak boat transom with the name *Andrada* cut into it. Canadian and American shippers identified the salmon as part of the cargoes shipped on the *Andrada* and *Ardnamurchan*, and they were sure that some of the cases found on the beach were from the bottoms of the ship's holds. This excluded the possibility that they had been thrown overboard to lighten ship. Cargo from the bottom of a ship's hold comes out only when unloading is complete or when in some fatal disaster the hull has split open.

The mills of government ground slowly but at last orders came for the revenue cutter *Grant* to search the west coast of Vancouver Island. Coaxing a sufficient head of steam into her venerable boilers, the long-suffering engineers, late in January, put out to sea. The following is a report of their findings as printed in the Tacoma *Ledger*:

"Feb. 11, 1901: The revenue cutter *Grant* returned this morning after one of the most important and dangerous cruises ever undertaken by a vessel of that service in the Northwest. Captain Tozier has been searching primarily for some evidence that would lead to an explanation of the British ship *Andrada*, which, after arriving off the mouth of the Columbia River, was blown offshore many weeks ago and never heard of since . . . The *Grant* made the entire circuit of Vancouver Island, standing off and on the savage coast, and at Marmanah the Indians had a ship's name board bearing the *Andrada* name, which they had picked up on the rocks.

"Indians and a trader at Clayoquot Sound told Captain Tozier of a big ship sighted Jan. 24 a few miles offshore and on her beam ends, with seas breaking over her. There were no signs of life and the surf on the beach was too high for the Indians to go out at the time, but the next day several canoes put out. The big ship had disappeared and after 12 hours' search no trace of her was found. . . . Capt. Tozier says the west coast of the island is well called the Graveyard of the Pacific Northwest. Most remarkable discovery was a three-masted vessel high and dry on a beach three miles from Clyoose Village. There is no record of the stranded or of the fate of the crew, and Indians say it has been there a long time. Heavy surf prevented the *Grant's* landing a boat."

Although not due at Liverpool for two months, the *Andrada* was given up as lost. Her reinsurance rate, now set at 90 per cent by Lloyds, meant that the underwriters had abandoned any hope of her safe arrival. At the same

time a 70-guinea premium was offered to anyone willing
to reinsure the *Ardnamurchan,* another concession of
disaster. In this unusual case both ships were given up as
lost before they could even be listed as overdue.

Some theorists decided that, in the darkness and sleet
of a December gale, the two big clippers had crashed and
gone down together. Since they had sailed at about the
same time and their wreckage had been so thoroughly in-
termingled on the Graveyard, this theory was as logical
as any other. It was not revised until much later when,
battered and leaking, the *Ardnamurchan* turned up off
the Irish Coast. That left the riddle of the *Andrada*
deeper than ever, for she never did appear. Only the lit-
ter of wreckage on the Graveyard hinted at her tragic
story.

These are the cases that left traces of a sort. Having
met their fate close to land, they cast ashore some revealing clues. The stories of those that perished far from
shore have beginnings but no endings. Briefly their pyra-
mids of canvas rose off Flattery, then dropped below the
horizon, or were blotted from sight by in-sweeping storms,
and they were seen no more. They left no trace. The best
that can be hoped for such ships is that their crews died
quickly. And they probably did.

FOR MANY YEARS THE STEAMBOAT was the principal means of transportation between the cities and towns of Puget Sound. In 1853, the first local passenger steamer, the tiny side-wheeler *Fairy,* arrived on the inland sea, and the boat routes grew and expanded steadily until about 1915. Then, as new highways were pushed along the winding shoreline of the Sound, the motor car and motor bus began to take over. By 1935 local passenger steamship service on Puget Sound had practically ended; today there is no regularly scheduled passenger steamer in operation anywhere on this vast inland waterway.

Only two of the once-great fleet of inland steamers are still in commission. Formerly the *Virginia V* and the *Sightseer* (ex-*Vashona*) were scheduled boats between established ports. Now they operate only in the summer months, running as excursion steamers out of Seattle. The rest of the Puget Sound steam fleet is gone. Most of the little ships were scrapped but a few were converted to ferries to serve the automobiles that put them out of business.

In its heyday this flotilla of small steamers, which numbered in the hundreds, was called the Mosquito Fleet. Its ships developed into two distinct classes. On the sheltered reaches of the upper Sound the river-type stern-wheeler was much in favor. In appearance, the salt-water paddlers differed from the famous river boats—they seldom went in for the gingerbread and gilt trimmings—but their general anatomy was the same. They had shallow hulls, drawing very little water, and the leverage of their big wheels and multiple rudders clear aft made them easy to maneuver. Seldom did the stern-wheelers get into serious trouble. They operated in waters that the fury of ocean storms could not reach. True, they frequently stranded in fog or darkness, but they just relaxed on the beach until the next high tide, when the big wheel, back aft in deep water, usually succeeded in pulling them off. The flat, shallow hulls took kindly to the gravelly beaches of the upper Sound and none of the paddlers were ever involved in a really serious stranding. In the rare instances when winter ice formed on the shallow bays they navigated, they had an answer for that too. They just turned around and backed into it, the big paddle buckets of the stern-wheel pulverizing all the ice they could reach.

Fire was the greatest hazard to the stern-wheelers. The *Walsh*, the *Vashon*, *Annie M. Pence*, *City of Stanwood*, *Despatch*, *Ellis*, *Fanny Lake*, *Fairhaven* and *Messenger*, all went that way. Sometimes a dignified stern-wheeler like the *Multnomah* or the *Harvester* was rammed and sunk by a fast-moving steel-propeller steamer; but, over a 65-year period, the leisurely old boats managed to cover millions of miles carrying millions of passengers without killing any of their paying guests.

During the steamboat era, propeller steamers dominated the lower Sound routes, and many of them were in operation on the upper Sound as well. The typical Mosquito Fleet propeller was long and narrow, with an enclosed boiler and freight deck extending the full length of the hull. Above this came the many-windowed passenger cabin, topped off by pilothouse and texas, funnel and lifeboats. Every vertical line had a smart rake aft and the little ships had an attractive, sturdy look about them. Actually, many of them were not as sturdy as they looked. Competition was keen and the fastest boat got the business. To insure speed they were built with knife-narrow hulls and were sponsoned out above for added space. After they were launched, enough gravel or slag ballast was shoveled into their holds to prevent their lying over on their beam ends.

Then they were put to work. They always raced with, and sometimes ferociously butted, opposition boats, rarely slowing down for wind, wave or fog. On the smaller boats the skippers often acted both as purser and freight clerk, leaving the navigation largely to the mate. In spite of these lighthearted practices, the steamboats enjoyed a remarkable safety record. In the eighty-year history of the Mosquito Fleet, fewer passengers were killed than in an average four-month period on the state's highways.

Two or three Mosquito Fleet disasters, however, stand out in history. The foundering of the *Clallam* in 1904 and of the *Dix* in 1906 were major tragedies.[1] Within a few months of each other, both steamers were launched at Tacoma and both suffered reverses at their launchings which old-time sailors considered sure portents of disaster. The *Clallam's* sponsor missed the bow with the luck-bringing bottle of christening champagne. Then as the new ship slid down the ways her flag was broken out upside down, and the *Clallam* took to the water flying

1.—Full details of these wrecks are in the companion volume to this book, *Ships of the Inland Sea.*

the symbol of marine disaster, a reversed ensign.

Early the following year, while en route from Port Townsend for Victoria, she was overwhelmed by a gale in the Straits of Juan de Fuca. Her engines were flooded out and she drifted helplessly all night. The women and children were drowned when the boats were lowered and many of the male passengers perished when the steamer capsized and sank after the tug *Richard Holyoke* had a line aboard. All told, fifty-one lives were lost in the wreck of the *Clallam*.

The *Dix,* a smaller steamer, refused to be launched at all. She struck on the ways and had to be pulled into the water by a tug. Afterward she ran between Seattle and Alki Point, but, in the fall of 1906, was put on the Port Blakely route. On November 18, she left the Flyer Dock, for her night run to the mill town, headed out into Elliott Bay, then south on a course parallel with that of the Alaska steam schooner *Jeanie,* which was close off her starboard beam. Suddenly the *Dix* turned abruptly to starboard, directly across the bows of the larger ship. The steam schooner was moving slowly and her engines were reversed before the collision occurred. As a result, the two ships came together quite gently. The *Dix* was not structurally damaged, but the *Jeanie's* bow pressed the top-heavy little Sound steamer over until her port rail was under water. Inrushing water simply engulfed the *Dix* and within a very few minutes she sank stern first.

The *Jeanie* picked up many of the passengers on deck but those in the cabins had no time to get out. The *Dix* went down in a hundred fathoms, carrying forty-five victims with her. Only one body was recovered. The rest still probably inhabit the dark cabins where they died. After a lapse of almost half a century the exact cause of the tragedy remains unknown, for mate Charles Dennison, who swung the wheel to send the *Dix* speeding across the *Jeanie's* bow, went down with the steamer. He was the only man in the pilothouse and no doubt he still keeps lonely vigil there.

Other Sound steamers met violent ends, but in the process they seldom killed their passengers or crews. Sometimes luck seemed to be very much with them, as in the case of the passenger steamer *Alice Gertrude*. The little Black Ball liner carried passengers, mail and freight from Seattle to Neah Bay, stopping off at such way-points as Port Townsend, Port Williams, Dungeness, Port Angeles, Port Crescent, Gettysburg, Pysht, Clallam and East Clallam. On her outward trip, the night of January 11, 1907, she ran into heavy weather in the straits. At eight o'clock in the evening in the face of a rising gale, she had left East Clallam. After about two hours, Captain Charles Kallstrom concluded that his ship was making very little headway in the teeth of the storm and, in the process of getting nowhere, was taking an undue beating.

Accordingly, he turned about and headed back toward the shelter of Clallam Bay. By this time the gale had become a howling blizzard and the shore lights had been blotted out in a thick blanket of snow. The ship's officers strained their ears to catch the hoot of the fog signal at the bay entrance and the lookout in the bows brushed the stinging, wind-flung snow from his eyes as he tried to catch the glimmer of the entrance light. Apparently the fog horn was not working that night and, when the lookout sighted the light, the steamer was only about two hundred yards off the beach. The engines were reversed at once, but too late to save the ship. A big swell picked her up and slammed her down hard on an immense whale-backed rock offshore.

For the next half hour the passengers and crew underwent a terrifying ordeal. Completely lost in the wind-whipped snow and tossing seas, they had no way of calling for help. Every swell that rolled in sent the *Alice Gertrude* crashing with sickening force against the big rock that had trapped her. With her hull ripped open, the ship

settled on the rock and lay comparatively quiet. Until
then her people had expected her to go entirely to pieces
at any moment, but this development brought new hope.
They carried blankets and bedding to the smoking room
and all stayed with the ship until dawn. Then the wind
went down and with it the snow. Soon after daybreak the
big ocean tugs *Lorne* and *Wyadda* sighted the distress
signals from the *Alice Gertrude*. Everyone was safely transferred to the tugs and taken to Seattle. Steamboat inspectors, as well as his passengers and crew, commended
Captain Kallstrom for his coolness and prompt action in
the emergency. The old *Alice Gertrude* was a total loss,
but like most of the Mosquito Fleet ships, she died like
a lady, dragging no one down to disaster with her.[2]

The list of such wrecks is fairly long. Some of the
Sound steamers expired dramatically by running aground
at full speed or by getting themselves cut in two in the
fog, or by going up in great pillars of fire. Seldom, though,
was anyone seriously hurt. The *Yosemite, Nisqually,
City of Kingston, Calista, Kitsap, Athlon, Eastern Oregon, Perdita, Telegraph* and *North Pacific* were only a
few of the Mosquito Fleet sisters that sank or burned in
various and spectacular manners, but without taking
human life.

Its safety record rather than its disaster roll is the most
remarkable thing about the Puget Sound Mosquito Fleet.
The little ships carried their millions of people to and
from a hundred harbors along the shores of the inland
sea. They carried them somewhat slower than the modern automobile, but they carried them safely. Puget
Sound steamboats could probably boast of a lower death
rate than any other transportation system in modern history; but this is an age of Progress and they are all gone
now.

2.—She did, however, give her crew a good scare. Witness the statement of A.
G. Roberts, her steward. He was a veteran of nine shipwrecks and had spent
eleven days in an open boat when the *Hindustan* went down in the Far Pacific, but he avowed that the wreck of the *Alice Gertrude* on inland waters
scared him more than all nine deep-sea disasters combined.

THE JADE BUDDHA

LEGENDS AND THE SUPERSTITIONS
of the sea are many and varied, though in this age of
mechanized seamanship and eight-hour-a-day seamen,
they are fast dying out. At almost any cost, the old-time
shellback avoided a Friday sailing and he refused to allow
a preacher on his deck. All Finns were considered war-
locks who could summon a hurricane at will, and stick-
ing your knife into the base of the main mast and whistling was believed a sure way of bringing wind to a becalmed ship. It was bad luck to change a ship's name and
to run across the Flying Dutchman off the Cape of Good
Hope meant certain disaster.

Legend has it that in the days of the "wooden
walls," the British Navy tried to put an end to some of
the sailors' pet superstitions, particularly the one about
Friday. Picking out a staunch sloop-of-war, they renamed

her H. M. S. *Friday,* placed a Captain Friday in command, and dispatched her on a cruise on Friday the thirteenth. Neither ship nor crew was ever heard of again.

So it is that ancient sea lore refuses to be wholly stamped out. Take, for instance, the case of the Jade Buddhas. Any early-day sailor will tell you that a Jade Buddha in a ship's cabin is more dangerous than nitroglycerin in the hold. The story that follows concerns a couple of the little heathen idols and the trouble they caused. It is told by a sailor who knows and loves the sea, Ralph Cropley, a veteran purser on North Atlantic liners. Many of the famous ship models in the collection of the late Franklin D. Roosevelt were the work of his hands. He has spent half a century gathering sea lore and his collection in the Smithsonian Institute is one of the largest of its kind in the world. At an age when most men in swivel-chair jobs are thinking about retiring, Ralph Cropley is serving as a ship's officer on a navy transport running between the West Coast and Korea. Between voyages he told the story of the Jade Buddhas and, when we asked him to put it in writing for inclusion in this book, he did. He wrote it in the middle of the Pacific Ocean and mailed it from Japan. Here it is in his own words:

THE JADE BUDDHA

"Sailormen of the old school have ever been filled with a wide range of superstitions as to what affects the welfare and destiny of their ships. The superstition I have in mind to tell about has to do with a figure of Buddha in jade. Why Buddha? I think it's more the jade than the Buddha that brings bad luck to sailormen.

"Anyway, Captain Arthur Brown, the last master of the famous *Mauretania,* had an unhappy experience with a small jade Buddha. He was then master of the Cunarder *Franconia,* which was making a world cruise. At an official dinner in Hong Kong, a Chinese of high degree insisted on the Captain's accepting a tiny Jade Buddha, an exquisite bit of carving. Knowing the superstition of the sea concerning a Jade Buddha, the Captain tried to refuse, even though he really wanted the figure for his wife. But nothing doing. The Chinese insisted and Captain Brown had to return to the *Franconia* with it, fully intending to give it away in the morning and get it off the ship. The *Franconia* had enjoyed excellent luck on her world cruise, and he wanted this to continue until he got her safely back to New York.

"Much to his later chagrin, by the next morning Captain Brown had forgotten all about the Buddha. The *Franconia* sailed for Japan with the idol still aboard. Within half an hour after dropping her Hong Kong pilot in clear weather, she not only had stuck her nose into a dense fog but had run down a Chinese coastal steamer!

"As Captain Brown told me about it, over a gin and bitters when he got back to New York, it was not until after the collision that he had remembered the Jade Buddha. To prevent the cussed thing from causing any more trouble, he went to his cabin, grabbed it out of a drawer, rushed out on deck, and flung it as far as he could into the dense fog. That done, the fog immediately began to clear.

"His telling the story recalled my own experience with a Jade Buddha, which I had purchased around 1909 in a curio shop in Vancouver, B. C. That figure was to cause the *Princess May* many years of misery. Because of it she changed from a well-behaved ship to a perfect rebel, kicking up the very devil. Why the sudden change? Well, during a cruise in Alaskan waters I lost my Jade Buddha on the *Princess May*. How or why I wasn't to know for another ten years when, at the Todd Yards in Brooklyn, the *Princess May* was being converted to bring Jamaican negroes north as government laborer. Behind the old-fashioned washing contraption in the cabin I had occupied years ago, a Todd workman found that Jade Buddha I had bought in Vancouver.

"Apparently a roll of the ship had sent it to the floor, then slid it out of sight. How I happened to be there at the time, Heaven alone knows, but I was, and in uniform, and so I had the misfortune to regain my lost idol.

"And what about the *Princess May* during the ten years she had it? Folks about Vancouver and Seattle are quite familiar with the picture of her after the tide had fallen and left her balanced at a 23-degree angle with her midships propped up by the rock she had run aground on. And that was just one of many antics a once-respectable ship performed. But when Buddha was out of her system the *Princess May* again became almost saintly in her behavior.

"And that Buddha! Foolishly I kept it on my next voyage and that is how, I fully believe, I came to spend ten days in a lifeboat in the middle of the Atlantic. Yet, I assure you, that Buddha wasn't in the lifeboat with me, or we'd never have made the grade. Before I left my sinking ship I did old Mother Atlantic a dirty trick by tossing the blooming thing in her bosom.

"Maybe that is why, when you get to 40 north and 50 west, your cabin ports are dark and green with the seas outside, and your ship shudders with restless, heaving old Mother Atlantic."

THE SCHOONER *NORTHLAND* GETS CAUGHT IN A TRAP

ALMOST ANYTHING IS LIABLE to happen to deep-sea fishermen. As a class, they expect the worst and so are seldom greatly perturbed when it happens. But one black night the crew of the fishing schooner *Northland* ran into a situation off the Graveyard that left them talking to themselves for a long time. They could not tell anyone else about it, because it was one of those embarrassing accidents extremely hazardous to the victim but highly comical to everyone else—like sliding on a banana peel or coasting into an open manhole.

On a July night in the year 1906, the *Northland* was inbound for Seattle from the Cape Scott Banks. There was no fog, but the heavens were black and starless, a heavy swell was rolling in from the general direction of Japan, and a strong summer gale was blowing. Well

107

reefed down, the graceful schooner was driving fast before the wind along the west coast of Vancouver Island, making for the Straits of Juan de Fuca.

The night was so dark that the shore was invisible, but the glow of the American and Canadian lighthouses and of *Swiftsure* Lightship showed Captain Contillion his position clearly enough. There was little danger of colliding with any ship whose navigation lights were lit, but to play doubly safe he was keeping the *Northland* well inshore and out of the steamer lane. One hand was on watch forward, another was at the wheel, and the Captain was on the quarterdeck.

Disaster struck the *Northland* quite suddenly. One moment she was bowling along merrily, the next she had come to a sudden, staggering and complete stop. With a horrible crash of splintered timbers, she had struck some solid object. This was followed by another rattle and thud as the main topmast hurtled to the deck, trailing a tangled mass of rigging and gear. Captain Contillion picked himself up from the deck where the sudden stop had deposited him, plucked a few of the larger splinters from his stern, and tried to size up the situation. It appeared that his ship had collided with some derelict being borne to its final resting place on the Graveyard.

But the skipper was wrong. The *Northland* had not run down the shattered hull of some unfortunate sister of the sea; nothing so romantic as that. It finally dawned on the unhappy mariner that he had simply run his ship directly into a large fish trap, and there his ship was caught, as securely as any blundering salmon.

Now, deep-sea fishermen have little use for fish traps, even when they are not caught in them. These traps—long parallel rows of stout piles extending from shore to deep water, like deckless piers—ensnared millions of fish that might otherwise have filled the holds of the fishing fleet. And the great sea harvest was taken by landsmen, who kept one foot on shore and took none of the chances of the ocean anglers. It can be imagined how the Captain felt about it when he found himself, his crew and his beloved *Northland* trapped in this one.

At the moment it was no laughing matter for any of the fishermen. Plunging and rearing in the heavy sea, the schooner was rapidly knocking herself to pieces against the upperworks of the trap and threatening to pierce her hull against the jagged fangs of broken piling. For hours the men worked overside in the boiling surf between the pitching, towering sides of the schooner and the great, barnacle-encrusted piles. At last they got the ship untangled and managed to kedge her out of the fish trap. The *Northland* was still afloat but, along with her dignity, she had lost most of her spars and rigging.

Captain Contillion worked her into Seattle without further mishap and there the marks of her encounter with the fish trap were removed, but not forgotten. Though the Captain had considerable to say about Canadian trap operators who left their murderous contraptions unlighted and unattended, only part of his remarks were ever printed in the newspapers of the time. It is unfortunate that history does not record the exact words of that deep-sea fisherman when he first discovered that he was caught like a sockeye salmon in somebody else's oversize fish net.

If the sad case of the *Northland* failed to convince the skeptical that anything can happen to a fisherman, and probably will, the schooner *Libby* clinched the matter. This *Libby* put into Anacortes the following year minus her bowsprit and with her fore-rigging in a sad state. The crew explained in simple language that a whale had knocked it off but newspapers gave the occurrence more color. Headlines like the following appeared:

WHALE ATTACKS SCHOONER!

—

*Captain Christensen Tells of Encounter
in Which Vessel Escapes Capsizing by
Narrowest of Margins.*

—

*Submarine Monster Whips off Bowsprit
With Tail and Gives Craft a Terrible
Bump For Good Measure.*

Somewhere between the Nordic taciturnity of the crew and the hysterical headlines of the newspapers was the written report of Captain Christensen, submitted to the owners to explain the necessity for a new bowsprit:

"We were coming down from around Valdez Island and were just past the Sisters, some rock off Lasquetti. Johnson was at the wheel. Suddenly he threw it hard over and the schooner answered at once. I let go the main sheet just in time. Forward there was an awful splash, a thump on the step, then a swish in the water, and the next minute the bowsprit was gone, hanging only by a few stays. The jib was flapping loose. We had collided with a whale that had knocked off the bowsprit with his tail as he went down. The bow of the schooner struck him on the side as he was coming to the surface to blow. A minute earlier and we would have been lost; he would have come up directly beneath us and capsized the schooner."

Many of the old wind-driven fishing ships went missing with all hands. Perhaps one or more of them met the strange doom that the *Libby* escaped by such a narrow margin. If so, the story will never be told, for no one survived to tell it. But the strange adventures of the *Northland* and the *Libby* bear out the original contention—almost anything is liable to happen to a deep-sea fisherman.[1]

———

1.—Not fishermen, but pilots, were the victims of the only actual sinking of a ship by a whale, that the author knows of offhand. The San Francisco Bay pilot schooner *Bonita* was rammed and sunk by one off the Golden Gate about 1897.

THURSDAY, DECEMBER 6, 1906, was a day long remembered by sailors of the Northwest Coast. It ushered in a series of winter gales and near-hurricanes that swept the open sea and the inland waterways alike, and piled the beaches with the shattered timbers of wrecked ships and the sodden remains of jettisoned cargoes. At Seattle the wind began to rise early on the afternoon of the sixth; by evening it was blowing a full gale. Ships strained and plunged at their dock moorings, plate glass windows were pushed in by the mighty gusts, and streets were littered with telephone and light wires and fallen signs from the business buildings.

At Victoria the rampaging easterly wrought similar damage, and shortly after midnight a tremendous sleet storm swept down the great canyon of the Fraser, lashing the Strait of Georgia to new fury. Then the mighty

111

storm swung around and blew from the southwest, making a ravening lee shore of the Washington Coast and the Graveyard. On the morning of the seventh the storm was still raging, although with diminishing force. Newspapers carried accounts like this:

"No reports of disasters to shipping have been made; but it is feared that when communications are restored, news of shipwrecks will come in. The dangerous west coast of Vancouver Island would receive the full brunt of the storm last night, and if any sailing vessels were caught close inshore off the island, or the coast of Washington or Oregon, disaster would probably follow."

That was once the prophets were right, for tidings of disaster came in almost daily during the rest of the month, the first appearing the next day, December 8:

"Victoria: The government steamer *Quadra* arrived here tonight with Captain Allen and the crew of nine men of the bark *Coloma,* out of Everett with a cargo of lumber for San Diego. They were rescued from the wrecked and waterlogged vessel near Cape Beale. The *Coloma* met her fate in Thursday night's terrible gale. She was abandoned with masts gone, bowsprit broken away, decks awash and seams opened so that part of her cargo had floated away from the hull. Had the *Quadra* not come to the rescue in the nick of time, all hands would have been drowned. As it was, they had a very narrow escape from being lost with their vessel, now a hopeless derelict drifting toward the rocks near Cape Beale."

The crew of the *Coloma* owed their lives to a woman—Mrs. Thomas Patterson, the wife of the keeper at Cape Beale Light. After the old bark began to fall apart under the lashing of the wind and whooping seas, the men salvaged bits of cargo and planking, constructing a makeshift raft upon which they hoped to reach Vancouver Island in the morning. During the night, however, the raft was swept away and with it went their last hope of reaching shore alive. From the lighthouse tower at daybreak, Mrs. Patterson sighted the drifting wreck. Knowing that the *Quadra* had put into Bamfield Creek for shelter the night before, the courageous woman quickly donned oilskins and boots and began the five-mile trek through the pouring rain and screaming wind, over a trail knee-deep in freezing mud and slush.

Battered and exhausted, she at last reached the sheltered cove where she met the *Quadra's* captain coming ashore in a small boat.

"Quick!" she shouted. "A ship is going ashore near Cape Beale and the crew are all in the rigging!"

The Canadian skipper wasted no time. His boat rounded to and went slashing back to the steamer. It was hoisted aboard and the *Quadra* surged toward the open sea. Lookouts soon spotted the *Coloma,* her mainmast trailing overside, her bowsprit gone and her mizzen-topmast and topgallant crumpled on the deck. Her few remaining yards were sadly cockbilled and her battered hull was so low in the water that the tattered American flag streaming upside down from the stump of the mizzenmast was a superfluous mark of distress. The crew was safely transferred to the *Quadra,* the hulk of the old windjammer being left to the storm. Built at Warren, Rhode Island, in 1869, the *Coloma* was long past her prime; and when she piled her broken bones on the Graveyard, she probably saved some future crew from going missing with her in deep water.

On the same day, December 8, another storm-battered ship received attention, for her adventures indicated that helpless windships might not be the only victims of the storm. The Great Thursday Gale proved that it could slap the daylights out of even a big, modern steamer. The story went like this:

"Port Townsend, December 8: After a terrible experience with the elements, the steamer *Olympia,* under Captain Croskey, put back to port this evening with several feet of water in her hold and her deck cargo shifted to port. She had sailed on Wednesday from Everett for San Francisco with 1,500,000 feet of lumber. Thursday night at ten o'clock, when the vessel was a hundred miles south of Cape Flattery she was struck by a southwest hurricane blowing at the rate of sixty miles per hour. For some hours the steamer bucked the gale, but with engines running full speed forward no headway could be made.

"Enormous waves dashed over her, momentarily threatening to carry away her bridge and house and actually tearing the lifeboats from their fastenings and smashing them like kindling wood. At midnight Chief Engineer Wood informed Captain Croskey that water stood three feet above the platform in the engine room with the pumps being forced. Croskey concluded to heave to. This was accomplished with difficulty and only after oil was employed fore and aft.

"Heavy seas shifted the deck cargo until the vessel showed a fifteen-degree list to port. On her run to the straits much of the water was pumped out and pumping still continues. At this time the vessel has partly righted herself, still carrying an eight-degree list.

"The Northwestern Steamship Company, owner of the *Olympia,* has been notified. Captain Croskey thinks the deck cargo can be righted and the few repairs necessary made here. The vessel shows no leaks, all of the water having come in from above.

"Speaking of the gale, Captain Croskey says he fears that news of disaster to other vessels will follow."

The *Olympia's* skipper had seen what the awful storm could do to a steel-hulled, powerfully-engined steamship. and it is no wonder that he feared for the safety of the wooden windjammers and lesser steamers that had been caught offshore in the same gale. His fears were well founded. The next day the schooner *Roderick Dhu,* under Captain Anderson, arrived at Tacoma with fuel oil from Monterey. Her crew, with that of the tug *Dauntless,* which had towed her up the coast, had another spine-chilling story of a night-long brush with death.

The Thursday Gale had caught these ships off Cape Meares. Once a British-Australian immigrant ship, the schooner had been rigged down as an oil barge, carrying only a single foresail to steady her. At the height of the storm the hawser parted and the oil-filled schooner went wallowing off to leeward before screaming winds of almost a hundred miles an hour. When darkness fell, the

The Alaska liner *Olympia* stranded in Prince William Sound during a 60-mile an hour gale in 1910. Passengers and crew were saved, but the *Olympia* was a total loss.

Survivors of the *Valencia* being taken aboard the *Queen*.

The heavy ice crust on this Alaskan liner, the *Northwestern*, illustrates grotesque hazards of the northern sea routes.

The schooner *William Nottingham* and steam tug *Wanderer* now.

lights of the tug were soon lost in the scud and spray. Captain Anderson of the *Roderick Dhu* had this to say about the events of the next few hours:

"In the twenty-eight years I have been at sea I have never had as close a call as that of Thursday. In the frightful gale of December 6, at about 5 p. m., the wind was blowing at eighty-eight miles an hour. At 8 p. m., when the hawser broke, the wind must have been blowing a hundred miles an hour. It was impossible to stand on deck. The sea was running over forty feet high. With a howl the wind tore away the foresail, which was of new Number One canvas, the first time bent. It was a south-wester, hauling to west-southwest, and we were about ten miles off Cape Meares. At 9:45 p. m. the Cape Meares Light bore east by south 3/4 south, at the same time the Tillamook Light bore north by west. At 4 a. m. the schooner was anchored in thirty-three fathoms out on the port anchor and 120 feet of manila line on the starboard anchor. The sea was breaking all over the ship.

"We drifted fully 500 feet inshore toward the rocks after we dropped anchor. The men suggested that we put out a boat and go to the Meares Light, but after talking the matter over, I convinced them that the place for us was with the ship. If we had attempted to reach the light we would have been lost. As it was, I did not expect to see the tug again; I felt sure it had gone down.

"I, of course, ran up flags of distress right after we anchored. A white steamer with a yellow stack and black top passed us and I signaled her, blowing my whistle all the while, but she did not answer us. I suppose she did not see us, though I cannot understand why. With the aid of the oil pumped overboard we succeeded in holding all right until the tug came. It reached us about 9:45 a. m. on the seventh. Captain Darragh of the *Dauntless* and I feel that we have both been very lucky and hope for no more such experiences."

The Captains Anderson of the coastwise ships have never been noted for their oratorical powers and the fact that this Captain Anderson told such an eloquent story speaks volumes for the Thursday Gale. It stood out above all others in a life spent off the stormy Northwest Coast.

Much more could be written of the heroism of the men aboard the helpless *Roderick Dhu,* who stuck to their ship as she drifted relentlessly toward the spouting reefs;

and of Captain Darragh and his men of the *Dauntless,* who spent the night coasting the line of breakers until they found and saved the helpless schooner. But no amount of devotion and bravery could have saved the *Roderick Dhu* if she had been carrying coal, or scrap iron or even lumber. Her oil cargo made it possible to keep her off the beach. More than five hundred gallons were pumped overboard to flatten the sweeping graybeards that would have hurled the ship ashore. The oil gave the men a little more time and, just a few minutes and a hundred feet from the wet, black death of the coastal rocks, they pulled her to safety.

Another shipwreck was reported on December 9, when the tug *J. M. Colman* towed the schooner *Forest Home* into Port Townsend. On the day after the Thursday Gale, the schooner had picked up the crew of the American bark *Sea Witch* two hundred miles off Cape Flattery.

The *Sea Witch* was another of the decayed old craft sent west to carry lumber, on the theory that if they fell to pieces at sea their buoyant cargoes would keep them afloat. On December 2, she sailed from Port Hadlock, lumber-laden for San Francisco. The storm caught her on the sixth and tossed her around until she became unmanageable, her sails blown to shreds and her seams wide open to the sea.

Andersons are as numerous in the West Coast lumber fleet as Murphys in the New York Police Department; another Captain Anderson commanded the *Sea Witch.* He had taken his bride along for her first sea voyage and apparently she got her money's worth. By Friday night the decks were almost awash, only the lumber cargo keeping the bark afloat at all; and blue distress rockets flared from her sea-swept decks into the dark sky. On the horizon the *Forest Home* was standing in toward the straits in ballast, and her master—it seems his name was Captain Anderson —sighted the disaster signals from the *Sea Witch.* The big fore-and-after came scudding in before the wind and hove to off the waterlogged bark. More quiet, routine heroism ensued as the men of the *Forest Home* ferried the crew of the *Sea Witch* to safety, across mountainous seas and in the face of hurricane winds.

On the tenth of December word of another marine disaster reached Port Townsend when the schooner *William H. Smith* brought in the crew of the British ship *Manalope,* Eureka to Tacoma, wrecked off Cape Blanco. The gale hit her, setting her on her beam ends; her ballast, seven hundred tons of wet sand, shifted and kept her there. As she slowly filled, the eighteen men of the crew, along with Captain Wills, his wife and two daughters, took to the rigging, where they remained throughout a most unpleasant night. In the morning, after four hours of still more unpleasant work, a boat was got out on the sea-swept deck, and the passengers and crew abandoned the apparently sinking ship. Later, the steam schooner *Northwestern* towed the derelict into Astoria. The ill-wind that had left her helpless blew considerable good to the steam schooner men, who collected a sizable piece of salvage money to enrich the waterfront saloon keepers.

On the eleventh, another fierce gale swept in, with a 61-mile-an-hour wind velocity recorded at Seattle. Breaking loose from her moorings, the hulk of the old German steamer *Mariechen* went careening around Elliott Bay in the dark, narrowly missing the British ship *Marion Josiah,* anchored in the bay, and finally crashing into the Army Transport *Dix,* moored at a dock. Next day, news of damage inflicted by the big storm of the sixth was still trickling in. The barkentine *Amelia* was towed into Port Townsend, badly battered but still afloat. Some freak of wind and current had borne her to safety through hazards that had killed hundreds of other ships. Outbound from Astoria to San Francisco, she was caught by the Thursday Gale off the mouth of the Columbia. With every stitch of sail blown away, she drifted helplessly toward Cape Flattery and the lee shore of the Graveyard that lay just beyond.

Windships caught in this predicament did not escape unless some steamer sighted them and hauled them to safety. The *Amelia* was never sighted. A freak current and an inshore draft of wind caught her off the mouth of the straits and carried her to the calm water inside. Many fine ships had made the silent pilgrimage up the North-west Coast to the Graveyard and the *Amelia* seemed as much a victim of that relentless drift as any of them. Some whim of fate caused her to take a detour through the narrow gate to safety.

Although her crew had escaped from the sea, they almost died of hunger within easy sight of the fat dairy herds ashore. The barkentine had taken twenty-seven days for a voyage supposed to last five, and her galley was bare of food. Finally a tug sighted her, gave her food, and put a line aboard. Tug and tow made Clallam Bay before the December 10 gale struck, and the next day, with tattered rigging and a half-starved crew, the lucky ship *Amelia* reached Port Townsend.

On the thirteenth the famous old Alaska gold-ship *Portland* put into Seattle, followed on the nineteenth by the *Pennsylvania*. Both steamers had been long overdue, having fought gale after gale all the way to and from the Far North. Snow particles snatched from the glaciers by the howling wind had added to the hazards of their voyages, creating a white curtain as dangerous as fog, and much more uncomfortable.

With the Alaska liners accounted for, there was hope that the last had been heard of the Thursday Gale, but not until December 29 was the final victim reported. On that day the bark *Andrew Welch* put into San Francisco with the survivors of the American full-rigged ship *Great Admiral* aboard.

The *Great Admiral* was another old-timer, Boston-built in 1869. For several years she had been sailing as a coastal lumber carrier out of Puget Sound and on De-

cember 1, 1906, she left Mukilteo, fully loaded, for a
routine voyage to San Pedro. Then, like the other ships
whose routine was sadly interrupted by unkind fate, she
was caught in the Thursday Gale. Her captain's log tells
her story in the simple language of the sea:

"Dec. 6: Position by observation, latitude 46:43 North; longitude 127:58 West. This day comes in with wind and sea increasing and hard-passing squalls.

"6:00 p. m.: Wind and sea still increasing. Sea now continually
breaking over the vessel.

"6:30 p. m.: Noticed ship settling in the water and, upon exami-
nation of the well, found vessel rapidly filling with water, it now
being up to within 24 inches of the between-decks. Immediately
ordered fire to be made in the donkey boiler and start main and
steam pumps, but engine room found to be partly flooded and
boiler under water. Seventeen inches of water taken in during
ten-minute period.

"7:30 p. m.: In order to try to save the vessel, cargo, and lives
of crew, if possible, we cut away the main and mizzenmasts with
all attached. Ship now all under water and sea breaking furiously
over her with top of after house just awash onto which all the
crew, including the mate's wife, have taken refuge."

"With wreckage of main and mizzenmasts hanging alongside,
the ship came round on the other tack, carrying away the jib
boom with all attached, causing the foremast to fall overside.
Ship now a complete wreck with top works and deck load washing away.

After that, Captain Sterling had no time for keeping
the log. A tremendous sea swept the old square-rigger
from stem to stern, snatching off the roof of the after
house and flinging it, with its clinging mass of humanity,
far to leeward. Battered by timbers from the cargo, the
cabin roof broke in two and the eighteen men and one
woman clambered aboard the largest section.

There they clung all night, with hail squalls lashing
their wet bodies and great combers sweeping clear across
their flimsy raft. The cabin boy, a frail child, suffered
terribly from the freezing cold and the ship's cook tried
to shelter him in his arms, from the worst of it. The gray
light of dawn disclosed both dead of cold and exposure.

Because the bit of wreckage was overloaded, sometimes two feet under water, and the living could not spare room for the dead, the bodies of the cabin boy and the cook were put overside.

Little Mrs. Catherine Martin, the first mate's wife, proved again that women are as likely as men to become sea heroes. As the long day passed in cold and terror, she kept the will to live burning in the men. By nightfall the gale was still blowing and hissing; icy waves still swept clear across the raft. There was nothing to eat or drink and faces and hands were blue and wrinkled with the cold. Everyone but Mrs. Martin had given up hope. She cheered and encouraged the rugged seamen, who drew strength from her words. When a sailor went mad and tried to hack his own throat and wrists with a rusty pocket knife, she tore strips from her dress with which the others bound him.

At daybreak the haggard survivors of the *Great Admiral* peered with bloodshot, salt-rimmed eyes over the vast, gray expanse of ocean and saw a white square lifted above the tossing horizon for a brief moment. Then it rose again, the upper foretopsail of a square-rigged ship. As the oncoming ship pushed on up over the curve of the world, the exhausted people on the bit of wreckage saw the lower base of her canvas climb into sight. Next they could see the hull as it lifted to the rushing seas, shouldering acres of white foam to either side. The square-rigger headed directly toward them. If only she kept this course before she sighted them! Captain Sterling had a few rockets in a water-proof wrapping and he took one out now. A sputter and hiss and a long stream of colored fire arched into the sky. The oncoming ship loomed closer and closer and then, with the creaking of backed yards and the booming of canvas, she was heaving to. They had been sighted.

It was the British Cape Horn square-rigger *Barcore*, outbound from Puget Sound for Australia. Her boats came yawing across the tumbled, gale-whipped ocean and took the spray-whitened, half-frozen crew off the wreckage to the safety and comparative comfort of the *Barcore's* after-house. A Horn-rounding limejuice windjammer had few luxuries, but the crew of the *Barcore* fought each other to give their blankets and food and warm clothing to the sufferers from the Yankee ship. On Christmas eve the victims were transferred to the homeward-bound *Andrew Welch,* and five days later they landed at San Francisco.

Young Mrs. Martin was deeply grateful to the men of the *Barcore*. "May God bless every one of them," she said, and she was speaking for all hands from the *Great Admiral*. A giant, tattooed foremast hand from the sunken ship summed up how the *Great Admiral's* crew felt about their first mate's wife:

"If it hadn't been for the little missus we would have every one been at the bottom of the Pacific this minute. She seemed full of hope when all the rest of us *wanted* to die."

And so the great Thursday Gale passed into history, having done tremendous damage to ships and cargoes, killed surprisingly few seamen, and made heroines of two women—the wife of a lighthouse keeper and the wife of a mate in sail.

Properly the story of the storms of December, 1906, should end here; but, to gain perspective, it is interesting to note what was going on aboard the ships that were safely in harbor when disaster struck their sisters at sea. Were the harbor crews tense and anxious, thinking of their friends fighting for their lives in the grip of the awful storm? Probably not. Not if the lumber schooner *Polaris* was any criterion. By the skin of her teeth she had beaten the storm into the straits and was safe and secure at an Everett mill dock. But all was not well aboard the humble lumber yacht. One hundred pounds of rancid butter lay in the galley. It had been there five months and the crew refused to go near it, let alone eat it. The captain vowed that no more butter would come aboard until they *did* eat it. But the crew caught him sneaking two firkins of sweet, fresh butter aboard for his own use.

Caught between captain and crew in the bad butter controversy, the steward finally fell in with a mutinous plot of the foremast hands. He switched butter on the captain. The skipper ate some of the crew's butter in an onion and salami sandwich which was strong enough to blot out all other odors. As a result, he was taken violently ill and expected to die. The crew stood around gleefully to watch him do so, adding to ironic justice by telling him what the steward had done. However, the captain had a strong constitution and survived the poisonous effects of the crew's butter. The mate took the schooner into Puget Sound, while the skipper was confined to his bunk. The steward lived in deadly fear of the full recovery of the captain, who had solemnly promised to kill him as soon as he was able to walk again.

When the *Polaris* reached her haven, the crew did not kneel in gratitude at their deliverance from wind and wave; instead, they watched the unhappy steward race a flung belaying pin to the dock and sprint up town to file a complaint with the Deputy Shipping Commissioner. Then they observed the skipper blunder to leeward of the galley, get a whiff of the 100-pound lump of butter, and stagger, retching, to the rail. Rude men of the sea that they were, they clapped each other heartily upon the back and rolled about the decks in unseemly merriment.

If the *Polaris* had been a little slower sailing up the coast, the Thursday Gale might have made heroes of her men, giving them a chance to snatch victory from the snarling sea like the men of the *Roderick Dhu* and the *Amelia*. As it was, they only managed to snatch victory from their stingy skipper with his rancid butter. But, human nature being what it is, they were probably happier about their exploit than were the real heroes of the great storm.

THERE HAVE BEEN worse shipwrecks on the Northwest Coast than that of the Pacific Coast Steamship Company's liner *Valencia*, worse as to total lives lost and number saved. The *Pacific* and the *Princess Sophia* claimed more lives. None escaped from the *Sophia* and only one from the *Pacific*, while nearly forty survived the ordeal of the *Valencia*. Nonetheless this wreck achieved a unique pinnacle of horror. At least those who went down with the *Pacific* off Cape Flattery, or took the last plunge with the *Sophia* over Vanderbilt Reef, died quickly. The sea was comparative-

123

ly merciful to them, their time of terror and agony being brief. Yet the sea showed what it could do in the way of refined cruelty when it took the helpless ones of the *Valencia*.

The sailing of a doomed ship on her last tragic voyage is no more dramatic than any other departure. Only in retrospect can we see the clouds of a grim fate gathering about her as she clears the harbor and drops the landward marks astern. Certainly the young woman in the apartment at the north end of Powell Street in San Francisco had no premonition of disaster, and her full attention was centered on such a ship.

The apartment's living-room window overlooked Meigg's Wharf and the bay, and that was a wonderful thing for a sailor's wife. To her, a husband's time in port is a precious commodity. By living where she did, Mrs. Johnson could cheat the sea of a few extra moments of that cherished time at the beginning and again at the end of each voyage.

It was exactly five minutes to eleven on Saturday morning, January 11, 1906, when Mrs. Johnson stood at the window with her little daughter to get a final glimpse of her Captain. Down below, his ship, the *Valencia*, was trailing a cloud of black smoke from her tall funnel and white steam was fluttering at the stack safeties. The canvas-sided gangplank was coming inboard, and Captain Johnson had just opened the pilothouse door and stepped out on the bridge.

She felt her usual thrill of pride when she saw him, tall and handsome in his gold-trimmed uniform, taking his place of command. In twelve years' service with the Pacific Coast line he had gone up from quartermaster to master of as fine a liner as plied the coast. Mrs. Johnson thought a little pride in her man was justified, and she pointed him out eagerly to the little girl who climbed on her lap, anxious to start the "game they always played with Daddy."

In the watery January sunlight they watched steam blossom from the great, shining brass whistle and, in a second or two, heard the mournful, spine-tingling call of a departing steamer's last whistle blast. Then the lines dropped from the dock bollards and a strip of water grew and widened between ship and pier. The liner *Valencia* was free of the shore.

"Daddy! Daddy!" the little girl shrilled, waving wildly from the open window. The Mother smiled. Only a very small girl could expect to be heard at such a distance. But when, as always, the *Valencia's* Captain turned and waved his personal farewell to the shining window of home, she could not forbear her own, "Good-bye, darling, and God bless you and bring you back to us," which was more foolish still, for it was whispered.

Captain Johnson turned abruptly from his last glimpse of home, the window with its two small waving figures, to the ship's business. The safe delivery of the *Valencia*, her cargo, and the 154 souls aboard her, to Victoria was his sole responsibility now, and that left no time for dreaming.

The watery sunlight of the bay turned to drifting vapor off the Farallones. Off Point Arena the vapor became a heavy, solid mass of fog, which stayed with the *Valencia* all the way up the northern coast of California, Oregon and Washington.

Even when the waters and the coast line have the familiarity of twelve years of close association, dead reckoning is tricky business. Captain Johnson seldom left the bridge. By Monday evening his figures told him it was time to start groping for the entrance to the Straits of Juan de Fuca. Both the sounding machine and the deep-sea lead were put to work at six o'clock. By nine that night no bottom had been found with 240 fathoms of line. At ten the leadsmen sang out "sixty fathom," and the Captain guessed the ship's position as a few miles south of Flattery, probably in the vicinity of Umatilla

Reef. He ordered the course changed to north by a half east.

A little later the course was altered again—north by three quarters east—for the Captain was sure they were safely clear of the *Umatilla* Lightship and could start edging in toward the straits. The fog was thinning a bit so that it seemed possible at times to pick up the loom of land through the rifts to starboard. At ten-thirty the lead still showed sixty fathoms, but Captain Johnson was cautious, ringing the engines down to half speed, then to dead slow. The ship was creeping up the coast at four knots with the depths being called every fifteen minutes.

But the *Valencia* was not where she seemed to be. Heavy rains inland had swollen both the streams emptying into Puget Sound and the Straits of Juan de Fuca, causing a "set" out to sea. The northeast wind that was blowing the fog away combined with the incoming tide and the rain-swollen flood from the straits to create a powerful tidal current against the west coast of Vancouver Island, the Graveyard. This relentless ocean river gripped the steamer and swept her northward much faster than the Captain had predicted. The patent log was none too dependable, having been known to "overrun" the ship by as much as six per cent.

At a quarter to eleven the lead showed eighty fathoms; at eleven, sixty; at eleven-fifteen, fifty-six; at eleven-thirty, thirty-three. When the next sounding indicated that the water had shoaled to thirty fathoms, the Captain stepped to the engine room telegraph. Suddenly the big steamer shuddered and almost stopped. She had brushed an outlying rock and then shaken herself free. Bells jangled down below and the screw lashed the dark waters to foam as the wheel was put hard over and the ship's bow swung west, toward the open sea and safety.

But the Graveyard would not allow so fine a prize as the *Valencia* to escape. While the ship was completing her turn, her bow crashed heavily on a rock reef.

"My God, where are we?" cried Captain Johnson. He slashed the engine room telegraph to *full astern* and the mighty thunder of the reversed screw shook the length of the steamer. But it was biting deep and true, and the power of steam might yet beat the ocean. The officers gripped the bridge rail until their knuckles were white. Could the mighty backward thrust of the engines pull them, stern first, from the very jaws of disaster? Yes, it seemed that they were going to make it. Shuddering and protesting, the *Valencia's* hull slowly backed seaward from the reef's embrace, and was free. Unless the stout hull had been ripped too badly by the rocks, all were safe.

For a few minutes terror changed to thankfulness. The water showed no rise in the holds. Captain Johnson called the chief engineer on the speaking tube to ask if there were water in the engine room. Before the chief could answer, the engine room crew came boiling up on deck. They answered the Captain's question. A solid wall of water had chased them from both boiler and engine rooms.

Then Captain Johnson did the only thing left to do. His ship having swung around until it was headed back toward the open sea, he called for full speed astern. Chief Engineer Downing, still at his post with the in-rushing water rising to his waist, responded to the last signal from the *Valencia's* bridge. The reversed screw beat the water again, striving for the shore instead of the sea this time; and the ship drove back upon the reef it had almost escaped. Captain Johnson had faced the last, bitter decision of a shipmaster. He could beach the ship or let her sink under him. He chose what seemed the lesser of two evils.

What happened after the liner struck for the last time is best told in the words of one who was there, Frank Lehm, the *Valencia's* freight clerk, who was one of those who survived. The rising wind had become a yelling storm as the ship struck; and, ironically, the fog that had lured the ship to her death was blown away as soon as the damage had been done. The lifting fog revealed the ship's bleak position. The reef that had impaled her was only about thirty yards from shore, but what a shore! Sheer rock cliffs towered a hundred feet above the ship's deck, and there was no beach. Great graybeards broke across the wreck in a welter of dirty foam, then dashed against the cliffs with the rumble of thunder, exploded, and shot white water eighty feet up the rock face. There was, said Lehm, complete confusion among the passengers after the ship struck and the great seas began to sweep her deck. He recalled the following grim scene:

"Screams of men, women and children mingled in awful chorus with the shriek of the wind, the dash of the rain, and the roar of the breakers. As the passengers rushed on deck they were carried away in bunches by the huge waves that seemed as high as the ship's mastheads. The ship began to break up almost at once and the women and children were lashed to the rigging above the reach of the sea. It was a pitiful sight to see frail women, wearing only night dresses, with bare feet on the frozen ratlines, trying to shield children in their arms from the icy wind and rain."

Captain Johnson, accepting tragedy with courage, set out to salvage as many lives as possible. His voice rang out strongly over the storm and the cries of panic; officers and men rallied to his call and the first hysteria was followed by a period of desperate but purposeful activity. The Captain ordered the port amidships boat swung out. As it hung from the falls, a great comber swept it away, part of the boat crew still clinging to it.

"Lower the port quarter boat!"

The crew fell to manfully, and the boat swung out on the davits. Another great mountain of water crashed over the ship, and the lifeboat was crushed like an eggshell against the ship's side.

"Clear away the starboard quarter boat!"

Working with the fury of drenched demons, between seas, the crew got the boat clear and lowered it to the saloon deck rail. Officers were ready with drawn revolvers to back up their grim order:

"Women and children first!"

But the time of panic was past. Fathers said good-bye to wives and children and helped them into the boat, then stepped back to the listing, wave-swept deck. The dangling boat, jammed with women and children, was outlined for a moment against the sinister black cliffs and leaping spray, as the ship's searchlight held it in its white gleam.

"Lower away!"

On an even keel, with men fending it from the ship's side, the crowded boat began to drop toward the water. Then came a chorus of screams from its occupants. The stern fall had broken, or been cut, and the boat's stern plunged downward to the water's edge, the bow still suspended high in the air. A stream of humanity poured from the boat into the dark, foam-crested breakers. A few pallid, upturned faces showed in the searchlight's glare, then all was over.

To return to the words of ship's clerk Lehm:

"Again we heard the strong voice of the Captain, touched with tears, 'Get out the amidships boat!'

"The boat was filled with more women and children and safely launched. Oarsmen's faces were contorted as they strove to pull away from the ship's side in the boil of surf and the undertow from the cliffs. At last they started to forge ahead. A great cheer for those who were to be saved went up from the hundred left on board. Even the faces of the terrified women in the little boat looked more hopeful as they began to clear the wreck.

"We all thought them saved when suddenly a great breaker, larger than any I had ever seen, aided by a terrible gust of wind, struck the boat, slewing her around in spite of all that the man at the steering oar and the sailors could do. The next moment she was overturned.

"What a sight! The searchlight showed every detail of the terrible tragedy — the men and women struggling in the water, their faces ghastly in the glare; eyes that stared at us unseeingly, already glazed with the touch of death; the bodies of children

swept toward the terrible rocks, in a wild chaos of boiling surf.
Suddenly all of this vanished, the searchlight revealing only a
tossing, rolling, terrifying rush of water."

The Captain decided to keep the two remaining boats
aboard until daylight. Throughout the night rockets
were fired because the ship carried no wireless apparatus.
The steward portioned out blankets and a little food,
and those who still lived waited out the long, awful night.
The rising water killed the fires in the boiler room. The
electric lights, dimmed, flickered, and went out. The
living clung only to the dark shell of a dead ship.

A gray, storm-swept dawn revealed little to cheer them.
Surf still dashed high up the face of the lowering cliffs.
Bodies of the drowned were still there, first dashed against
the brutal rocks and then drawn out toward the wreck on
the undertow. No sign of help came from the sea or the
cliff tops above them, but after a while voices were heard
from the shore. Two or three men had escaped from the
wrecked boats and were trapped in a sea cave at the cliff's
foot. When the rising tide blotted out the narrow strip
of beach, they tried to climb the sheer rock wall. Halfway
up they lost their hold, falling, shrieking, to join the
floating dead.

The two remaining boats were cleared away, but after
that night of horror the remaining women refused to
enter them. Some attempt was made to carry them bodily
into the boats, but this was given up, and, instead, two
boats' crews went in search of help. Without the crowd-
ing weight of frightened passengers, the two boats won
free. One, with the boatswain and five men, was to try
for a landing on the beach. Then the crew was to find a
way to the cliff top where they could secure a lifeline
fired from the steamer's Lyle gun. The other boat, with
nine men, was to make for Cape Beale Light Station and
summon aid.

The boatswain's boat could not make a landfall until
they had rowed eight miles west of the wreck. Then they

spotted a telephone line on shore and followed it to the light station. The other boat landed at the telegraph station fifteen miles from Cape Beale. First news of the disaster reached the outside world by telegraph from the Cape Beale light keeper. Shore parties from Cape Beale found their way to the cliffs above the wreck, but never succeeded in making a line fast from the ship. Rescuers from the sea did little better.

At Victoria the liner *Queen,* the old *Queen of the Pacific,* just in from California, discharged her passengers and raced back toward the wreck. The big tug *Salvor* foamed out of the harbor in her wake. At Seattle, the *City of Topeka,* with steam up, loaded doctors, relief supplies, and newspaper men for the dash to Walla Walla Reef. The U. S. Revenue Cutter *Grant* was at dock in Seattle, but her skipper had not received orders from Washington, D. C., to go to the *Valencia's* aid, so he issued shore leave passes to most of the crew and had the fires pulled so that the engineers could putter with the leaky boilers! Such procedure in the face of the most horrible marine disaster in Northwest history will probably seem highly improbable to a present-day coast guardsman, but that's what happened in 1906.

It probably would have made no difference if the *Grant* had joined the other rescue boats. No deep-draft ship could help the *Valencia* victims and there was no surf boat available. By the twenty-fourth, the wreck was almost completely broken up, only the mast and funnel being visible in the breakers; but at least thirty tortured human beings still clung to the tattered rigging. It seemed part of the sea's fiendish whim to dangle salvation before their eyes, and then withdraw it. After the first impact the *Valencia* had almost won free of the reef, only to crash back, stern first. Next, the lifeboats made their gallant try, only to be crushed and sunk. Then the shore parties came to the cliff's edge and the Lyle gun sent the lifelines arcking toward them, but the gale swept all except one away. The last one, made fast to solid land, broke at the first strain put upon it. After that the *Queen* came rolling in; also the *Salvor* and the tug *Czar*—more hope for the battered, freezing people lashed in the *Valencia's* shrouds.

But there was no way to approach the wreck from the seaward side and the stunned watchers there saw the smaller rescue craft steam away, one by one, as their skippers sized up the futile situation. The *Queen* kept up the vigil, cruising offshore all through the night and till noon of the twenty-fifth. Her people had watched the pitiful figures in the *Valencia's* rigging droop and disappear, until only the shredded lashings and a few still bodies dangled there. Then the wind, its work done, began to moderate and the seas grew less murderous. The little steam whaler *Orion* arrived and was able to run in close to the reef. It confirmed, beyond a doubt, that all life had ended on the *Valencia.*

Later in the day the *City of Topeka,* coming out to relieve the *Queen* on the deathwatch, picked up a life raft with eighteen half-frozen survivors who had left the *Valencia* the previous morning. Another raft, launched at the same time with ten men, came ashore on Turtle Island in Barkley Sound, but only four survived. Five of the men reached shore raving mad and soon cast themselves back into the sea. The others were saved by Indians.

When the score was totaled, it was found that 117 had perished with the *Valencia;* only thirty-seven had been saved. Captain Johnson, of course, stayed with his ship and her helpless passengers until the end. The little girl on North Powell Street never completed her "game with Daddy." The game was never won until the *Valencia* came steaming proudly through the Golden Gate and Daddy saw her waving from the seaward windows, and that was not to be again.

The *Valencia's* death helped to bring about many reforms: radio on ships, lifesaving stations to patrol the

Cape and the Graveyard,[1] and an unsnarling of the red
tape which had made the revenue cutter service impotent.
And that just about ends the *Valencia's* pitiful saga—
unless you like ghost stories. . . .

After the water had closed over the sunken liner and
117 of her people, the *City of Topeka* steamed back toward Seattle with the handful of survivors she had picked
up. Off Cape Flattery she spoke the *Queen,* outward
bound on her regular run. The *Queen's* searchlight
focused on the inbound ship while news of the wreck and
the survivors was exchanged. The wind blew the black
smoke from the *Topeka's* stack in a driven cloud to leeward. There, dim and transparent in the murky smoke,
ghosted the wavering outline of a steamship, an outline of
the vanished *Valencia.*

Later cool heads explained that it was a simple optical
illusion, that the people on the *Topeka* had seen the
shadow of their own ship, which was a near sister ship
to the *Valencia,* reflected on the drifting smoke bank by
the searchlight of the *Queen.*

But there were those aboard the *City of Topeka* that
night who will tell you to this day that they saw the
Valencia's ghost out between the Graveyard and the
Cape.

1.—The first lifesaving station, an experimental one, was established by the
government about twenty years before the *Valencia* disaster. A former territorial governor of Washington, Dr. W. A. Newell, secured, while serving as
U. S. Senator, a $10,000 appropriation to construct the station. It was not
until well into the twentieth century, however, that the present widespread
and efficient lifesaving service came into being.

PASSENGERS ON THE NORTHERN PACIFIC trains between Portland and Seattle get their first glimpse of the quiet reaches of Puget Sound when the train flashes out of the evergreen forests and snakes along the winding shoreline of Nisqually Reach, Cormorant Passage and the Narrows. For a few minutes they see the shining expanse of island-studded waters as did the passengers of the old-time Sound steamers. Then the train rumbles into the blackness of a tunnel and out into the Tacoma railway yards, back into the familiar world of carbon monoxide, billboards, neon signs and smog.

Those who glance up from their newspaper or canasta hand long enough to view the shoreline, as the train speeds through that brief, beautiful vista, may notice the hulks of three ancient ships rotting away on the mudflats

134

of Nisqually Reach. The junkies have had their way with them and there is little charm or dignity left to them. They would not impress the casual traveler, these old dead ships; but, to those who knew them in their days of life, they are silent and melancholy reminders of the great era of sail and steam on the Northwest Coast.

One such ghost ship was the fine old deep-sea steam tug *Wanderer,* well known for sixty years from Flattery to Olympia. Another was once the graceful three-master *John A.,* schooner of the West Coast codfishing fleet, and a third was the *William Nottingham.*

The *Nottingham* was a big four-poster schooner, built at Ballard for the Globe Navigation Company in 1902; and, like many of her sister wind ships, her adventures would fill a volume of its own. She was a Cape Horner. Not many fore-and-afters could claim knowledge of that grim, storm-swept corner of the world, where the big square-riggers were often hard pushed. She served under the American and Norwegian flags and ended her days with stubbed-down masts, as a cable barge for the Puget Sound Power and Light Company. Never again will she lift to the sea. Her battered hull is broken open and filled with drifting sand where the quiet tides creep in and out of her wounds. Now only the crying of the sea gulls breaks the silence of her abandoned decks. But forty-five years ago, it was far different with her.

On a late June day in 1906, the trim schooner *William Nottingham* rode at anchor in Port Townsend Bay, her scanty crew busy battening down the hatches over seven hundred great Douglas fir trees. These trees had crashed from the tidal forests to the beach and, bereft of limbs and foliage, had been snaked by a tug to where the schooner lay waiting. The forest giants, many of them more than a hundred feet long and three feet in diameter, were carefully stowed, for they were Boston bound; and, in 1906, that meant they were going around the Horn. Now, as soon as the crimp's boat brought the rest of the crew aboard, the *Nottingham* was ready to sail. Few seamen were foolish enough voluntarily to sign aboard a fore-and-after for a voyage around the Horn with a cargo of logs.

The crimps brought their boatload of human misery alongside and the latest crop from the saloons and sailors' boarding houses was ready to go to sea again. But one big seaman refused to go. He had heard about the road the *Nottingham* proposed to travel, and he wanted none of it. Because the captain had paid the crimps their blood money, he owned this seaman; for in those days men were still drugged and slugged and sold into sea slavery. This particular sailor felt it was better to get killed quickly in a break for liberty in Port Townsend Harbor than to take his chances off Cape Horn; besides, he had a knife. In his simple difference of opinion, he wanted to go overside.

The captain meant to keep him aboard. The sailor's rusty knife bit four times straight into the captain's back before that officer sank down, dirtying his sanded quarterdeck with his own blood. The mate's belaying pin knocked all dreams of liberty from the sailor's head and the disagreement temporarily reached a stalemate. But the "old man" was only twenty-nine and very strong. A doctor patched up his punctured back and the police took the sailor ashore to the Port Townsend jail, which was preferable to the fo'c'sle of a Cape Horn schooner. Taking a line from the steam tug *Wanderer*, the *William Nottingham* was drawn toward Cape Flattery.

Two months later she sprang a leak off the west coast of South America; the donkey engine stained the sails with black coal smoke while the steam pump clanked day and night. The pumps kept the water down and she bowled on southward toward the cape.

It was late in September before they reached the latitude of the Horn and the ship was still leaking. Running for the Horn in week-long gales, pressed down by the gray, liquid weight of the racing sea-mountains and the mighty wind, the ship leaked worse. More water, seeping through the tarpaulins and caulking, found its way into the holds. The men were half frozen, half starved, and completely exhausted; but the *William Nottingham,* shouldering the Cape Horn rollers aside, raced on before the westerly gales. Then came a graver danger than water in the holds—ice!

Cape Horn is well within the ice belt, and ice gives the sailor no chance. He cannot see it. He has no searchlight, no radar screen. He can only run on before the westerly gales and trust to luck. If that is against him, he has made his last port. Ice gives no warning, so the *Nottingham* had none. She simply crashed head on into a tremendous frozen island ten miles long. Her foreyard crashed to the deck. Then ton after ton of shattered ice cascaded down the sheer, frozen face of the berg to bury the whole forward part of the schooner. Its crushing weight forced her head down until both the bowsprit and then the fo'c'sle were submerged. That was one way the Cape Horn ice killed the windships: pressing them down so that the great seas might sweep them clean, smash in their hatches, and sink them like stones, while the watch below still slept in their bunks.

Nothing ever survived from a ship sunk like that— there were never the bits of wreckage that drift ashore in kinder latitudes to tell of a ship's fate—for, on the decks of a windship rounding the Horn, everything was lashed down.

That is the way the *William Nottingham* was meant to go, but she refused to die. The water that flooded her fo'c'sle floated some of the ice away, the crew fighting and clawing at the rest until it too was gone. The steam pump clanked on, as it had for three months, while sodden, frozen men turned to the hand pumps. Clear water gushed from the scuppers day and night, but the four-master schooner fled on before the westerly gales. For seventy-two hours she played tag with the ice mountains off the Falklands. Then she rounded the Horn, leaking worse at every gale.

A few days before Christmas the *Nottingham* was picked up by a tug off Sandy Hook, which was six months out from Puget Sound by way of Cape Horn. She was towed up the coast to Boston, where she unloaded the biggest cargo of lumber ever brought around the Horn. After a few repairs to hull and rigging she picked up an oil cargo and headed for Sydney, Australia. Wanting no more of the *William Nottingham,* the crew that took her around the Horn jumped ship at New York. But the mates stayed on. This voyage would be a Sunday excursion, a simple jaunt around the Cape of Good Hope. Even they, however, admitted no appetite for more Cape Stiff ice and gales in a leaky schooner loaded with logs.

Five years and no one knows how many sea-miles later, the *Nottingham* again turned up off the Pacific Northwest Coast, again refusing to die after her crew gave up all hope for her. Caught in the fierce gales that swept the coast on October 9, 1911, she was dismasted and water-logged off the Columbia River. With decks awash and her tall masts surging alongside in a snarl of rigging, she was deserted by her crew and left to sink. The schooner *David Evans* picked up the crew and the *William Nottingham* was written off the books.

Days later a bar tug sighted the dismasted wreck and put a line aboard. Wallowing helplessly, almost invisible under the combers that swept clear across her, she was towed over the bar and into the harbor of Astoria. The crew of the tug collected salvage money for their efforts; the *Nottingham* was repaired, re-rigged, and put back into service for another generation and more.

They say that some ships, like some men, have fighting hearts and so cannot be conquered. The *William Nottingham* was such a ship and she was never beaten by the sea. But now she is piled up on the beach, as dead as any ship that ever stranded on the Graveyard or went missing in the outer reaches of the Pacific. To help form a breakwater for barges and log booms, a tug deliberately nudged her ashore. Ordinarily this would have deprived her of a place in a book about shipwrecks, but she was a good ship, a brave ship, and she should not be entirely forgotten.

If you ever ride the Northern Pacific along Nisqually Reach, look for the ghost of the William Nottingham. *You will see her with the ghost of the steam tug* Wanderer *at her bows, the way it was forty-five years ago off Flattery, and if you have a feeling for ships and the sea you may want to tip your hat to what is left of the four-masted topsail schooner* William Nottingham.

"LATEST ADVICES from the North indicate that the wreck of the American bark *Star of Bengal,* bound from Wrangell to San Francisco with a cargo of canned salmon, is one of the most heart-rending disasters that has occurred on the Pacific Coast in years. Previous advices that 110 men, including 15 whites, lost their lives are confirmed. Appalling scenes were witnessed while the struggling men attempted to swim ashore."

The Pacific Northwest newspapers were guilty of no exaggeration when, on September 24, 1908, they opened their page-one lead stories with such a paragraph. To this day, the wreck of the *Star of Bengal* remains one of the most tragic marine disasters in the annals of the Pacific Coast.

The ill-fated ship was built in Belfast at the famous

140

yards of Harland and Wolff. She was an iron square-rigged ship, 262 feet long, of 1,877 tons net register. In later years, under Hawaiian registry, she lost the yards on her mizzenmast to become a bark. She retained this rig when taken over by the Pacific-American Fisheries as one of the fleet of big windjammers engaged in hauling the Alaska salmon pack to southern ports.

Late September of 1908 found the big iron bark at Wrangell, busily engaged in stowing the entire season's pack of the Wrangell Cannery, forty thousand cases, in her capacious holds. By Saturday, September 19, she was ready to depart for San Francisco. The huge load of salmon had been topped by several thousand big metal drums used to convey oil to the cannery. These were being returned empty. The hatches were battened down while more than a hundred cannery workers, mostly Orientals, found bunk space in the deckhouses and between-decks for the autumn trip Outside.

But the big windjammer could not just sail away from the Wrangell dock. Between it and the open Pacific lay a maze of islands and rocks and narrow channels, the middle reaches of the Inland Passage. A couple of the cannery tugs would put lines aboard the *Star of Bengal* and tow her through the dangerous waters of the Alexander Archipelago to the open sea. Away from the precipitous islands, pinnacle rocks, and millrace tides of the Inland Passage, the little steamers would cast off their lines and the bark would head south under her own tall pyramid of canvas. That was the plan, but it did not work out quite that way.

Presently the steam tugs *Hattie Gage* and *Kayak* fussed out importantly to take the *Star of Bengal* in charge. The weather was fine, a hard and profitable fishing season was over, and spirits were high as the tall bark swung smoothly away from the dock, heading south in the surging wake of the towboats. Everything went well although the day, starting in flat calm, dimmed out on the wings of a brisk

and rising wind. The tugs continued to draw the big
bark easily through the narrow channels between frowning snow-peaks and steeply sinister rock islands, the *Star
of Bengal* following cleanly, like the true lady she was.
The night wind was brisk, but not dangerous. Not yet.

Midnight passed. The wind increased, whistling now
through the bark's taut rigging. A nasty sea was kicking
up, causing the little tugs to labor heavily. The *Kayak*
was very light aft, her wheel and rudder often rising
clear out of the water at the crest of a roller. This made
her almost unmanageable as the huge bulk of the *Star of
Bengal* began to yaw and plunge at the end of the hawser.
By 2 a. m., the erstwhile brisk wind had become a storm.
Within another hour it had risen to a half gale. The laboring, straining tugs were in trouble. The *Star,* a perfect lady in Saturday's calm, was the opposite as she
wallowed under bare poles behind the two panting little
tugs.

Aboard the bark, Captain Wagner peered anxiously
through the pre-dawn darkness of wind-whipped spray.
Then he roared quick orders as he caught the phosphor-
escent glimmer of surf climbing unseen rocks close off
the ship's starboard beam. The fore-and-aft staysails were
quickly hoisted and sheeted home in the hope that their
pull might help the tugs in their dragging battle with the
storm. Seeing the glimmer of canvas astern, Captain
Farrer of the *Hattie Gage* swung the steamer's helm over
to claw hard to port. If he could get the bark on the starboard tack so that her sails would fill, he might yet escape
the spouting lee shore that lay so close aboard.

Slowly, reluctantly, the great iron hull swung to the
left, away from the deadly phosphorous of the beach.
As they began to feel the pull of the wind, the sails slatted
once or twice. While the helmsman fought the great
kicking wheel, the *Star* heeled over ever so slightly. No
longer just a dead weight at the end of a tow line, she was
beginning to fight for her life.

"We must be almost clear of Coronation Island," Captain Wagner shouted to his mate above the keening of the gale and the cracking of the filling sails. "If those tugs stay with us another fifteen minutes—a half hour at the outside—we can make the open sea under sail."

At that moment the line from the *Kayak* went slack over the *Star's* bow. It had broken, or been cut. The tug had been taking a terrible beating from wind and sea, as well as from the strain of the heavy tow rearing and plunging at the hawser's end. Like broken violin strings, her funnel stays and mast stays twanged and parted. Her boilers shifted. Seas were sweeping across her decks. If the funnel went by the board, the insurgent waves would pour into the furnaces, put out the fires and leave the tug helpless. Then, when the *Hattie Gage* changed course, the *Kayak* refused to answer her helm. One tug was pulling to the left, the other to the right. Looking to starboard, the *Kayak's* master saw the white fire of the spouting rocks; looking to port, he met the same disturbing sight. The lead showed only seven fathoms of water. It was clear that the big windship was dragging the tugs backward into a cove or bight, while the tugs, on opposite courses, were pulling against each other. The *Kayak's* master ordered the towing hawser cut. Then he ran for the open sea.

A few moments later the remaining line to the *Hattie Gage* was cut. The *Star of Bengal* fell helplessly off to starboard, her breath of steerage way lost. For a few seconds Captain Wagner could not believe that, in the teeth of disaster, he had been abandoned by both towboats. But he hesitated only briefly before ordering an anchor dropped and the sails furled. Shortly thereafter the second anchor roared out. The ship's backward progress was halted; the anchors were holding. Then blue distress rockets flared from the dark, plunging bulk of the *Star of Bengal,* but the tugs did not return.

For the next two or three hours, while the ship hung

there on the very brink of destruction, it appears the gale moderated somewhat. With dawn, the wind rose to a howling sixty-mile-an-hour gale. The anchors still held, yet time was running out. Tremendous hissing seas swept in to hammer the ship with relentless fury and send her reeling against the anchors' grip. Roaring on in welters of dirty foam, the breakers boiled high on the narrow strip of beach a few hundred yards from the ship, or exploded in awesome white geysers against the jagged rocks even closer aboard. The *Star of Bengal* had passed the sheltered northern end of Coronation Island and was lying off the bleak south tip, Helm Point. Sheer cliffs rose five hundred feet from the narrow beach, which was exposed to the full force of the ocean.

At 7 a. m., the Captain ordered breakfast served out to all hands. Then, calling the ship's company around him, he issued his last orders. He wanted a volunteer boat crew for the almost suicidal attempt to reach shore with a life line. If they failed, and he made it quite clear that it was a forlorn hope, it would be every man for himself when the ship struck.

Four men, whose names should be remembered, volunteered for the almost hopeless attempt to save the lives of their shipmates: Henry Lewald, Olaf Hansen, and Fred Matson, able seamen; and Frank Muir, a cannery cook. Somehow a boat was lowered and unhooked without swamping or being dashed to fragments against the ship's side. Then a huge, racing graybeard caught it, shooting it with the speed of a bullet toward shore. In the last line of breakers the hurtling boat was smashed to kindling against a craggy rock. The four brave men were lost to sight under tons of churning water. The ones aboard the bark turned hopelessly from the rail to await the end.

Suddenly a great shout rose from those who still watched the shore. A small, dark figure was crawling, inch by inch, away from the reaching white fingers of the sea.

Another appeared beside him; then another and another. They staggered upright to pull the end of the precious life line from the water. They made it fast to a gnarled tree. The ship was linked to shore with a thin line of hope.

But by now the anchors were dragging badly. The ship was being driven inexorably into the line of breakers. There was pitifully little space and so little time. At a quarter after nine the *Star of Bengal* struck the rocks.

After she struck, the disintegration of the great iron ship was amazingly rapid. Forty-five minutes after the first shock she was gone, only her mizzen-topmast protruding from the dark water where she disappeared. Yet in those minutes many lifetimes of drama and horror were enacted.

As the hull split open, the cargo was driven toward shore on the crests of the tremendous seas. Suddenly the breakers lost the appearance of liquid mass, instead becoming great, towering walls of wood and steel. Thousands upon thousands of salmon cases and heavy steel drums filled the sea. This pitching weight of wreckage was what killed most of the *Star's* people. Battered men would crawl ashore to lie gripping the sand with blue fingers, fighting the undertow and striving to gain a little strength. Then the next breaker would loom up behind them, carrying its tons of broken cargo from the ship. The wooden wall of packing cases would plunge downward, burying the helpless victim under a deadweight that crushed his body to a pulp.

Other men fought their way ashore by means of the life line, hand over hand, high above the raging sea and grinding wreckage. A lithe Japanese worker was almost to the shore, swinging along the high line, when the broken hulk of the ship suddenly keeled over toward shore. The slack of the line dipped nearly to the breakers. Then the wreck careened far over in the other direction, drawing the line tight as a bowstring, shooting the twisting body of the man, like an arrow, sixty feet into the air. The body plummeted down across the ship's taffrail, to hang there, a broken thing, until a great sea swept it away.

The four men who had reached shore in the boat were fighting the sea and the crushing mass of cargo as if it were a living enemy. Time after time they dashed into the grinding, seething inferno to pull some exhausted victim to safety before the next rumbling wave of wood and steel could break over him and crush out his life.

Afterward Captain Wagner wrote the following account of his own battle with the devil's brew of wood and steel and water between the wreck and the beach:

"When the final shock came, the *Star of Bengal* appeared to heave up her entrails in three sections. As I was thrown into the water I saw the midships beams of solid iron come out in a tangled mass. The force necessary to produce this is scarcely conceivable. So strong had been preceding gusts that a five-inch iron davit was snapped short off. After I was thrown into the water, any attempt to swim appeared ridiculous. As I struggled only to keep afloat, I was hurled shoreward among a thousand cases of salmon and hundreds of metal iron drums that constituted our cargo. I was practically unconscious when I reached the beach."

As the Captain was hurled on the beach, bruised and bleeding and unable to drag himself to safety, the four volunteers of the lifeboat crew spied him. They dashed toward him, but before they could reach him a wave of cases and drums had swept partly over him. The crew arrived only in time to pull him free from the next great towering wall of grinding cases.

Like some huge animal in its death struggles, the *Star* had been rolling and pitching fearfully. Now the struggle was over; the ship was gone. But her cargo still swept shoreward. Tangled with it were the bodies of struggling men, one moment lifted high on great waves, the next sucked down to go rolling and gasping along the ocean's bed, hurled against rocks and crushed by the blind

The schooner *C. S. Holmes* escaped the Graveyard in 1909, but returned there to die in 1950.

In November 1915, the Chilean square-rigger *Carelmapu* was swept to destruction on the Graveyard shortly after this picture was taken.

The *Admiral Sampson* was sunk in a blinding fog off Point No Point, August 26, 1914.

The *Princess Victoria*—3000 tons of speeding steel—rammed the *Admiral Sampson*, cutting her almost in two, just abaft the beam.

The *Princess Sophia* on Vanderbilt Reef.

Swept off the Reef by a northern gale, the *Sophia* shows only a tip of her foremast.
None lived to tell the story of her final hours.

The passenger liner *Yukon* was wrecked during a typical Alaska blizzard. Swirling snow, screaming wind, and 20-foot waves hurtled her onto a narrow rocky beach near Seward, February 4, 1946.

avalanches of salmon cases and steel drums. The beach was strewn with mutilated corpses and more were added with each crashing breaker. Horror piled upon horror—legless bodies, armless bodies, disemboweled bodies, and unrecognizable, crushed things that had once been bodies. Sometimes the cries of still-living victims guided rescuers to heaped mounds of wreckage, from which they pulled one more survivor.

For a few moments, as he was swept inshore, Olaf Peterson, the second mate, found a finger-hold in a crevassed rock. Battered and choking, he clung to it, crying weakly for help; but before the rescuers could reach him, he was swept off and buried under an overwhelming mass of wreckage. When they tore its tons of sodden weight aside, there was nothing left to remind them of the Norse giant they had known.

So it went, until the final survivors were pulled, exhausted and bleeding, from the shambles of the breakers, and the receding tide had cast up the last of the broken bodies. The *Star of Bengal* had sailed with 132 souls aboard. Just twenty-two lived to huddle around the driftwood fires on that grim and horrible beach. The Oriental cannery workers had suffered the worst casualty rate. Of seventy-four Chinese aboard, only two were saved. Seven out of twenty-one Japanese lived through the ordeal, while all but one of the four Filipinos aboard survived. Fifteen of the thirty-six white men were among the bodies strewn on the beach. These were buried in shallow, sandy graves, the bodies weighted down with some of the salmon cases that had killed them.

As the day wore on in numbing cold and horror, the gale began to abate. At last the tug could be seen through the mist beyond the breaker line. When the wind died out, boats were lowered from the tug to fight their way through the still-dangerous swells. They made it to the beach and began to take the survivors off.

The *Hattie Gage* had steamed back to Wrangell for

help. The United States cable ship *Burnside* was docked there, and when her commander heard the awful news he hesitated not a moment; he cabled to Washington, D. C., for orders.

The *Kayak* managed to save the few who were left from the wrecked *Star of Bengal*. These were taken back to Wrangell for first aid and rest. Because seamen heal quickly, by September 26, less than a week after their horrible experience, they arrived in Seattle, bruised, scarred, and weak, but with plenty of spirit left. Most of that spirit was directed against the tug masters who had cut the hawsers and run when the *Star* was in her extremity. Captain Wagner could speak only in a whisper, but he did not let that stop him. Here is a small part, a very small part, of what he whispered from his Seattle hospital bed:

"I attribute the entire loss of life and possibly the loss of the ship to the improper and inhuman conduct of the masters of the tugs *Hattie Gage* and *Kayak*. This is seen in the length of time the vessel clung to her anchors after she was cut loose on a lee shore by the tugs, and before striking; and in the action of the skippers who abandoned us after seeing our distress signals of blue lights and making no answering signals.

"Fifteen minutes more of towing, a half hour at the most, would have taken our ship free of the lee shore and into the Pacific where the stout vessel would have been able safely to ride out a severer gale. We were abandoned without a word of warning."

As he gained strength, the windjammer skipper lost none of his bitterness toward the tugboat men. If anything, his rage and scorn increased. He insisted that there had been a lull of several hours in the gale after the bark was cut adrift and got her anchors out; that the tugs could have returned and pulled her to safety during that time. His parting shot, when he left for San Francisco to report to his owners, left no doubt as to his feelings:

"Those two captains are criminally cowardly and will

have to answer to the authorities and to God for 110 human lives."

Of course, the towboat captains had their side of the story, too. They denied that the storm had died out sufficiently for a return to the abandoned ship. If it was so calm, why didn't Captain Wagner lower his boats and simply row ashore?

They insisted that it would have been suicide to have approached within a mile of the *Star* as she lay anchored on that spouting lee shore just outside the breaker line; that they stayed with her until the bitter end; and that, if they had stayed longer, they would only have succeeded in piling their own ships and crews on that deadly beach.

The pros and cons of this much-disputed case have never been fully settled. The only certainty is that the bark *Star of Bengal* and 110 of her people died on the sea-swept southern tip of Coronation Island. For a long time, Helm Point remained a grim reminder of that awful tragedy, strewn as it was with the broken wreckage of ship and cargo and ship's company. Weeks later a party arrived to search the wreck area for salvage. As the tide ebbed they saw two strange, white faces grinning at them from the breakers. When the water dropped farther they saw that these belonged to two more victims of the *Star*. The two bodies, pinned down by iron wreckage and the heavy salmon cases, had gradually been shifted by the sea's action until they were in a standing position, their feet firmly anchored.

Gulls and crabs and fish had had their way with them, but the two skeletons in oilskins still stood as ghastly guardians of the ship's tomb—a fitting end to the tragic fate of the *Star of Bengal*.

WORST STORMS ON THE
Pacific Northwest Coast in the early 1900's have been recorded than those chronicled here. In 1920, for instance,
a hurricane swept the seaboard between Cape Blanco
and Cape Flattery with winds of well over a hundred
miles an hour. The anemometer at North Head, near the
Columbia River entrance, blew away after registering
132 miles an hour. These later storms and hurricanes,
however, seldom resulted in shipwrecks. The full-pow-
ered steamers and motorships, which have replaced the
sailing fleet and the wooden steam schooners, carry
radios with which to receive storm warnings well in ad-
vance. They allow themselves plenty of sea room before
the storm strikes and are then prepared to ride out the
worst the sea has to offer.

It was the windships that usually fell helpless victims to
150

the waiting lee shore when winter storms swept in, for they had no radios to give notice of approaching danger, no power except that of their sails. To them, the frequent, sudden southeast gales were deadly, and the toll among them was always high during winters of heavy storms. The winter of 1909-1910 was especially turbulent. There was still a large fleet of sailing vessels—the barkentines and schooners of the lumber trade; and the square-rigged ships and barks of the grain fleet—calling at Puget Sound and the Columbia River. Even then, the windjammers' days were numbered; and the old days when the wreckage of ships on the Graveyard told its annual grim story of death and disaster were soon to pass.

The 1909 storm series began around Thanksgiving Day with a howling gale lashing the coast from Alaska to Cape Blanco, in Oregon. Huge waves were whipped up, making one long, white-spouting deathtrap of the beaches, headlands and reefs of the North Pacific and the Inland Passage. In Alaska the gray, smoking seas crashed high on the exposed reefs and rocks, battering the newly-erected government lighthouses along the shipping lane.

The Lincoln Rock Lighthouse was shaken to its very foundations by the rollers which exploded against it to climb upward and over the glass lenses at the tower's head. The keepers' house was swept away by solid walls of battering water. So were the storehouses, the boats, the supplies. The lower windows of the lighthouse were smashed in and water filled the rooms at the base of the tower. The keepers sought refuge in the lamp-room at the top of the reeling structure. There they had nothing to do but listen to the storm and the grinding of broken masonry at the base of the light while they wondered if the Lincoln Rock Light was to take its place with New England's Minot Ledge Tower, which toppled into the sea during a hurricane, dragging its keepers to the ocean's depths with it. They had no food, no water, and very little hope.

Fortunately for them, during a lull in the storm, the army steamer *Peterson* came poking down the channel. Seeing the dangerous plight of the lighthouse men, the ship's crew lost no time in going to their aid. Somehow they managed to remove them from the tottering lighthouse to the safety of the steamer's deck, then to the nearest telegraph station where they informed the Bureau of Navigation that the light was out on Lincoln Rock. The station had to be almost entirely rebuilt before it could be put into service again. Other coastal lights suffered less damage during that and ensuing storms of the months of November and December.

While the hungry and frightened keepers of the Alaska Lighthouse were being transferred to safety, the first big gale had swept on to inflict further damage off Cape Flattery. It caught the British bark *Matterhorn* off the mouth of the Columbia River. The big windjammer was outward bound from Portland with a cargo of barley for Great Britain. Barley is a tricky cargo, much lighter than wheat or most other bulk grains and giving little stability to the ship carrying it. It is also prone to shift suddenly in a heavy sea. Not long before, the ship *Brodich Castle* had gone missing with a similar cargo. It was thought that she had been caught in a violent storm—the light cargo in her holds failing to keep her steady—and that the cargo had then shifted heavily enough to capsize her. No one could be sure about the *Brodich Castle*, but that is exactly what happened to the *Matterhorn*.

The raging wind pressed her over until the barley fell away against one side of the holds. Then the ship went on her beam ends. She lay over on her side with her masts at times almost under water. For three days and nights she stayed that way, drifting north toward the Graveyard, while her crew, directed by Captain Salter, tried to get her righted. Under perfect conditions, this would have been a hopeless task; in the teeth of the sweeping gales and smashing seas, it was quite impossible.

After hours of agonizing, dangerous work below decks, two boats were hauled overside and it was decided to abandon ship. While the mate, steward and a seaman were in one of the small boats, stocking it with emergency rations and necessary gear, a great comber lifted the inert bulk of the ship high in the air, then, with a sickening lurch, dropped it into the trough. The great masts swung down with the roll of the ship; the yards, pointed toward the sea, plunged through the boat like giant spears, smashing it to pieces and killing the men in it.

That left twenty-seven men aboard the wallowing hulk, with one boat in which to make their escape. The storm raged on and the prospect was not a pleasant one, but soon there was no alternative. On the third day the bark *Matterhorn* surrendered to the sea. With a hiss of escaping air from the holds, she lay far over on her side, dipping her masts and yards under the sea and slowly raising her barnacled keel into the air. As she rolled, the crew scrambled down her side into the one remaining boat. They filled every inch of it. As the sea crests spilled in over the few inches of freeboard, there was barely room for them to bail. No one had time to give the *Matterhorn* a farewell glance when she finally lifted her swinging rudder high into the air and slid from sight below the breaking seas.

Captain Salter estimated that his ship had drifted to within seventy miles of *Umatilla* Lightship before she gave up the fight, so he headed the overloaded little boat in the general direction of the reef. As they labored toward the Washington Coast, the wind hit better than eighty miles an hour. How they survived is a miracle of the sea, but they did survive, and were sighted—after a 27-hour ordeal—by the lightship's crew. A boat was lowered to go to their assistance and with its help they made it to the lightship's side. Hoisted aboard, they were fed and cared for until the gale abated enough to transfer them to Tatoosh Island. Only then, by way of the cable to the mainland, was word received ashore of the loss of the British bark *Matterhorn*. Three men died with her. Skill and courage and amazing good luck saved the other twenty-seven men of her crew.

After that the wind whipped around to the southeast to catch the schooners *C. S. Holmes* and *Balboa*, and the barkentine *Mary Winkleman*. With seas breaking clear across their decks, the three sailing vessels were swept relentlessly toward the Vancouver Island shore. Close off the deadly line of rocks and breakers these ships found luck that saved them from sure destruction. The wind, suddenly swinging around to the southwest, drove them back out to sea, away from death that danced in white robes along the shore of the Graveyard. They were three days beating back against the wind to the straits, but no complaints were heard from the crews. They reached the safety of Juan de Fuca's Inlet under sail, the *C. S. Holmes* living to make her famous Arctic trading voyages to Point Barrow until World War II. Commanded by Captains John Backlund, senior and junior, she gained considerable attention in this trade, for she was one of the last of the West Coast windjammers to keep her sails and her colorful personality.

Young Captain Backlund, her final skipper, modestly says that she never was anything but an ordinary old lumber yacht, even in her heyday. However, when she had her brush with disaster off Vancouver Island in 1909, she was noted as a fast sailer, holding the record between Puget Sound and the Fiji Islands. In 1904, she had made it from Port Blakely to Suva in thirty-eight days. For a number of years her eighteen-day passage from Grays Harbor to Guaymas was also the fastest on record, unbeaten till 1908 when the schooner *Irene* made it in sixteen.

The Graveyard had to wait a long time to get another chance at the schooner *Holmes,* but the Graveyard is patient and always on the job. The army took the *Holmes* over for war service, during which time she saw such rough going that the young captain did not want her back at the end of the war. In the winter of 1950, she was in use as a barge. Only the stubs of her tall masts were left and she was drawn around by the nose at the will of a rumbling diesel tug. Her humble duties found her off the west coast of Vancouver Island when another December gale swept in from the Pacific, forty-one years after the storm from which she had so narrowly escaped. The hawser to the tug parted. This time she had no sails to help her claw seaward. She drifted helplessly toward the shore's veiled reefs and jagged rocks. Glad to be rid of her wallowing tow in the teeth of that December storm, the tug rumbled out to sea. Though delayed more than four decades, the schooner *C. S. Holmes* was destroyed on the Graveyard after all.

But back in 1909, the *Holmes* was not the only ship to escape by the skin of her teeth. The barkentine *Benecia* was battered down by the storm off Cape Flattery. Her deckload of lumber was swept overboard; her hatches were stove in. She was seen laboring heavily, most of her sails blown away, and with many feet of water in her holds. In fact, she was given up for lost after several days passed with no further sign of her, yet she finally made it into the straits under what was left of her sails. There she was picked up by the tug *Tyee.* The same brief lull that saved the *Benecia* brought a whole fleet of storm-bound windships skimming in like battered seagulls. Along with most of her sails, the *David Evans* had lost 150,000 feet of deckload lumber. The *Ocean Vance* had only spanker and jib left when she fought her way in past Flattery. The *Ruth E. Godfrey* and *Rosamond* got in somehow; still they would have drifted ashore in the straits if they had not been sighted by tugs. They had no sails left. By this time, fortunately, the government had put specialized lifesaving cutters in commission to replace the inefficient old revenue cutters. The *Snohomish,* one of the new ships of the lifesaving service, having put lines aboard the two drifting schooners, towed them to safe harbors.

The big Kosmos liner *Setos* followed the wounded schooners to safety, but even the steel steamship suffered a considerable beating at the hands of the storm. Her decks had been swept, leaving twisted stanchions and bent davits. Her cargo had also shifted and she came trailing into the straits like a sick duck, as thankful as the windships to find herself in the sheltered waters of the inland sea.

By that time shipping people were beginning to wonder about the four-masted schooner *Susie M. Plummer,* which had left Everett for San Pedro with a lumber cargo just in time to catch the full force of the gale off Cape Flattery. Not until late in December when the Great Northern liner *Minnesota* docked at Seattle from the Orient was there any report of her. The crew of the *Minnesota* had sighted the lumber schooner, waterlogged and abandoned, in latitude 49:20, north longitude 128: 30 west. The *Snohomish* and *Tahoma* cutters, sent out to search for the derelict and crew, returned without having sighted either. Then, on January 15, 1910, the drifting schooner was seen again at latitude 48:22 north, longitude 127:19 west. She had drifted right into the steamer lane of the transpacific liners to become a menace as well as a mystery.

Nine days later the derelict was spotted by the British steamer *Tees.* By this time she had drifted to within eight miles of Cape Cook, Vancouver Island. The steamer got a line aboard and tried to tow the deserted ship into port, but another squall swept in, the hawser broke, and the *Tees* had to run for shelter. With their quarry once more located, the cutters resumed the search, the *Snohomish* finally sighting her on January 25. With the southeast gale still rampaging, it was impossible to get a line aboard. The next day the sea-swept hulk was again sighted, but the sea was still too dangerous to risk closing with her.

On January 27, the *Snohomish* finally got a line aboard. Both anchors, which were hanging over the schooner's bows, had to be cut away. The deck was gone, the seams were wide open, and seas were breaking clear across the wreck. Only her lumber chargo was keeping the *Susie Plummer* afloat. It was impossible to tow the half-submerged wreck, which yawed violently at every sweep of the sea. The hawser soon broke under the strain. Still, the *Snohomish* could report her mission accomplished, for the wreck drifted into San Josef Bay where it piled ashore and broke up, no longer a menace to other ships.

But what of the twelve men of the schooner's crew? It was assumed that they must have been picked up by some ship not equipped with radio to report the rescue, probably a coaster; that they would be heard from after a few more days when the rescue ship made port. But the days became weeks, and all the coasters were accounted for. None had rescued the crew of the *Susie Plummer*. So, it was reasoned, the crew must be aboard a trans-pacific ship or a Cape Horner. Aware that a wooden ship carrying a lumber cargo is practically unsinkable, the men would never have left their ship unless rescue were at hand. Their schooner, built at Thomaston, Maine, in 1890, was oak planked and framed, and considered one of the stoutest ships of the coastal lumber fleet.

The weeks became months, and all the transpacific liners and the Cape Horners were accounted for. None had seen the crew of the abandoned lumber schooner. Nearly a year passed before all hope was given up, but at last there could be no further doubt. The schooner's crew had perished somewhere off Cape Flattery in the storm of December, 1909. Probably they had sighted another ship close by and lowered a boat to reach her before their own ship broke to pieces. Perhaps a rain squall swept in to hide them before they were sighted from the other

ship, and so they were left abandoned on the gray, angry
sea to be swallowed up by the foam-flecked bulk of some
liquid mountain.

All was conjecture, of course. No one knows with certainty why the crew of the schooner *Susie M. Plummer*
deserted the relative safety of their lumber-laden ship
in that December gale of four decades ago. The answer
is hidden in the enigma of the sea. The riddle of the
Everett lumber schooner, like that of the phantom ship
Marie Celeste, is one that will never be fully answered.

SOMETIMES THE OLD WINDSHIPS
managed to claw around Cape Horn by the skin of their
teeth, carrying their thankful crews to safety through storm
and adverse gales and drifting ice, seemingly cheating the
ocean of a sure victim. But old sailormen will tell you
the ocean is a vindictive wench and sometimes slaps a jinx
on such escaping ships, making them almost wish they
had found a peaceful resting place off the grim cape.
Take the case of the French bark *Cornil Bart*.

The *Cornil Bart* was a big, iron windjammer, 280 feet
long, of 2,243 gross tons, built in 1902. The autumn of
1911 found her off the Horn, out from Newcastle for
Puget Sound with a hold full of firebrick, coke, pig iron
and cement. The prevailing westerly gales that surge
across that dark corner of the world had plagued her, and

159

now the sluggish dead weight of her cargo pressed her down
to the sweep of the Cape Horn rollers. For a week she ran
with decks completely awash, fo'c'sle and galley flooded
out, all hands half starved and more than half mad with
hunger, fatigue and terror. Her foresails and staysails
were blown out and she came near falling off broadside
to the trough of the sea, which meant certain death. Her
lifeboats were crushed and washed overboard; still, this
was a minor tragedy, for they would have been of no use
anyway.

But the breakwaters and hatch covers held out against
the sea. Somehow the *Cornil Bart* fought her way around
Cape Horn and into the Pacific. Though the Atlantic
had been cheated of another victim, the French bark
must have carried the Cape Horn jinx with her when she
made her escape. As she crept up the coast of Washington
in the dark, pre-dawn hours, somewhere between the
Columbia and Cape Flattery, the jinx went to work. The
American schooner *Albert Myers,* gliding south from
Grays Harbor for San Francisco, fell in with the Horn-
rounding Frenchman off the Columbia River. The *Bart*
rammed the schooner, which drifted away into the night,
rapidly filling with cold, sea water.

The bark suffered bent plates and twisted rails, but
she finally raised Cape Flattery, was picked up by a tug,
and reached Seattle on December 8, 1911, just 166 days
out of Newcastle by way of the Horn. The boatswain of
the *Cornil Bart* was a large and short-tempered Frenchman named Ferdinand Reion, a man who dearly loved
red wine, or, for that matter, almost any other color.
After his nerve-racked experience off the Horn he had
an even greater thirst. The wine of Seattle was not the
wine of Bordeaux and of Marseilles, however, and seemed
to disagree with him. His disposition, never much to
boast about, became as sour as the foreign wine he was
forced to drink. Deciding to exorcise his displeasure on
the crew, he knocked two of them violently to the deck.

The rest, seizing handy belaying pins, drove the boatswain ashore.

Along the waterfront, Reion stopped in at numerous saloons and grog shops, but the wine continued to disagree with him. Late in the evening and burning with revenge, he returned to the *Cornil Bart*. This time he knocked down three of the crew. But the survivors were ready for him. Armed with clubs, knives, belaying pins and galley utensils, they surrounded him with the amiable intention of binding him hand and foot and throwing him overboard. Horrified, Captain Pierre Zooneyund watched from the poop, mentally scratching one boatswain from the ship's company. The mighty Reion, though, felled several more French seamen and bounded toward the poop, the crew in full cry behind him. Not having any particular love for the uncouth boatswain personally, the Captain had no intention of trying to save him from the outraged crew. With quivering beard, Zooneyund scuttled for the companionway, dived below and locked himself up.

Forsaken by the Captain, the boatswain went clambering up the mainmast. Only one man at a time could climb the ratlines after him but none cared to get within range of his massive boot at that dizzy height. So they formed a circle at the foot of the mast, performing a frenzied war dance around the fife rail, brandishing weapons and loudly calling the drunken boatswain such Gaelic phrases as *Essence of Ten Thousand Swine* and *Sacred Son of a Small Blue Onion*. While the boatswain sat in the crosstrees and occasionally spat upon the crew, the Captain hurried ashore to put in a riot call.

Helmeted Seattle cops drove the crew to their quarters, then coaxed the boatswain down out of the rigging and into the Black Maria. As soon as the law departed, the crew started drinking the departed boatswain's wine and fighting among themselves. Captain Zooneyund tore his beard and talked to God, then put in a second call for the police. A permanent guard was placed aboard the bark, a move which, for a time restored peace. After a while Boatswain Reion promised to be a good boy. He was released from jail and, all being quiet at the moment, the police guard was removed from the ship. That was a mistake. Reion took a few pulls from his jug, wiped his mouth and knocked down four seamen. When the mate intervened, Reion knocked him down too, then kicked him in the ribs.

Captain Zooneyund put in a third riot call. This time the French vice-consul felt driven to action on the theory that the wild antics aboard the *Cornil Bart* were giving *la belle* France a bad name on Puget Sound. He had Reion and the ringleader of the brawling crew deported to France on a French square-rigger then completing her cargo at Portland.

With the chief trouble-makers gone and a return cargo in sight, Captain Zooneyund felt that his troubles were over. But the Cape Horn jinx was not yet through with him. Before the bark could be shifted from her anchorage to the dock, a United States marshal visited her. It seemed the battered schooner *Albert Myers* had made port, although she was mostly under water, and her owners were slapping a libel on the *Cornil Bart* for butting her so violently on that dark morning off the Columbia.

So another ship got her cargo, and the *Cornil Bart* lay, with bickering crew and rusting sides, while her legal problems were settled. Finally she got rid of the libel and shipped a cargo, heading out on the Cape Horn road again. Her later history is unknown, but it is to be hoped that the Cape Horn jinx went overboard somewhere around 50 south and 65 west, to plague some other ship. Poor Captain Zooneyund and the *Bart* had already had their share.

THE INSIDE PASSAGE OF ALASKA
was in a pleasant mood on the morning of August 17,
1913. From cloudless skies the newly-risen summer sun
smiled benignly. Fresh green islands were reflected in the
narrow blue waters upon which they seemed to float.
Along the forested mainland slim waterfalls shone like
the quick strokes of a crystal pencil as they dropped from
glacial heights. The scene was just what it might have
been before the first white explorers visited those northern waters—with one exception. The exception was the
passenger steamship *State of California*, north bound up
Stephens Passage from Seattle for Skagway.

Like most of the Alaska steamers, the *California* was
a veteran of the sea. Built at Philadelphia in 1879, she
was a single-screw iron ship of 2,276 gross tons, long familiar on the Puget Sound-California route of the Pacific

163

Coast Steamship Company. With the arrival of newer and faster steamers to fly its house flag, the company had transferred the old iron steamer to the northern run. She had left Seattle on August 13, 1913—a questionable sailing date for those of a superstitious turn of mind—and she carried a capacity load of passengers. A sensational new gold strike had been made at the Shushanna diggings; a small edition of the Alaska Gold Rush was on.

By the morning of Sunday the seventeenth, the *State of California* was nearing the territorial capital of Juneau and ninety miles of steaming would put her in that harbor. But there was another brief stop to be made first. A new cannery had been built the year before at Gambier Bay. The Pacific Coast Steamship Company had agreed to put the cannery wharf on its port of call list. The steamer eased into the calm water of the bay, her deep whistle blast echoing sonorously from the timbered mountain shores. With a jangle of bells in the engine room, the brief thunder of a reversed screw and the gentle creaking of dock piling, the S. S. *California* was docked at Gambier Bay.

A couple of cannery employes, a hand logger or two, a bit of freight, and a sack of mail were dropped at the settlement. Then the cargo boom forward was swung in and secured, and the gangplank was slid back aboard. The whistle bellowed again, the echoes rolling and reverberating around Gambier Bay. The mooring lines came snaking in, the steamer's bow swung away from the dock, and the *State of California* was headed out toward the passage and the northern ports.

Watchers on the dock and the cannery tugs saw the black smoke roll from her stack as the stokers fed the furnace fires. The green-hulled, buff-funneled steamer made a pretty picture as the beating propeller picked up its beat and the creamy bow wave piled up against the blue water. Then, abruptly, the pretty picture went grotesquely wrong. It was as if the action of a handsome travel film in technicolor were suddenly frozen by a broken projector. The background was still there, as bright and smiling as ever, but the center of interest, the swift-gliding steamship, was suddenly a dead thing. Her slim bow rose briefly, then dropped suddenly. The creamy bow wave was gone. Her movement stopped as quickly and as finally as though she had rammed into a great invisible wall. It was a moment or two before the ripping, tearing sound of riven iron plates reached the shore-side watchers. For those few moments they did not realize that their pretty travelog had become a grim picture of disaster.

Captain Thomas H. Cann, on the steamer's bridge, was momentarily as shocked and incredulous as the people on the dock. The chart told him that he was in the center of a broad, safe channel with a good thirty-five fathoms of water under the keel. Nothing could have happened to his ship! But something had happened; and, in a matter of seconds, it was obvious that the *State of California* was sinking. Almost before the awful noise of the ship's death blow had left his ears, he felt her settling, going dead under him.

For many years, Captain Cann had commanded the steamer *Valencia*. When she made her last voyage from Seattle to San Francisco he had taken her in through the Golden Gate. Then he had turned her over to Captain Johnson, he himself being transferred to another of the company's ships. So it was Captain Johnson rather than Captain Cann who, in 1906, took the *Valencia* to her rendezvous with disaster on the Graveyard. Now, seven years later, disaster caught up with him. Like Captain Johnson on the *Valencia,* Captain Cann on the *State of California* had only one choice left. He must beach his ship.

He swung the wheel hard over. There was no time for verbal orders. He watched the bow swing sluggishly toward the beach. He felt the ship sag and wallow. Her whole bottom must have been ripped out on some huge, uncharted rock, and it was a question whether she would live to reach the shore, though it was only a few hundred feet away.

The screw continued its slow beat, forcing the dying ship toward the beach. White faced, the Captain felt a great thanksgiving as he heard the grating of the rocky shore under the keel and watched the bow climb high upon the beach. Passengers and crew, it seemed, were to be saved, even though the ship was finished. He turned quickly to supervise the loading and lowering of the boats. The crew worked fast and efficiently. Boat after boat was swung out, held briefly at deck level to receive its load of frightened passengers, then slid smoothly to the water alongside.

Cannery tugs and launches were racing toward the beached liner too, for although only two or three minutes had passed since the first alarm, Alaskans respond to emergencies with a minimum of delay. The whole drama was played to a tight schedule. A few hundred heartbeats saw it out from start to finish. As the boats took to the water, the ship's decks heaved, forcing the upperworks high above the buckled hull. Masts and funnel toppled and fell. A crashing mast struck and sank one of the crowded boats. The bridge and pilothouse were torn loose as a single unit and dropped overboard. On the bridge Captain Cann remained in command, though his place of authority had been violently removed from his ship. As the *California's* navigating section floated away on the tide, the Captain, on what was left of his ship, continued to roar orders and encouragement to his crewmen.

Then, without warning, the broken hull of the steamship slipped backward from the abruptly sloping beach into deep water. Almost in the wink of an eye she was gone, swallowed up under fathoms of surging, eddying water. Huge whirlpools formed above the sunken hull,

sucking down those who struggled in the water. Many of
these came back to the surface with some breath still in
their bodies. A good many did not.

Late sleepers were the principal victims of the sinking
of the *State of California*. Those who were awake, on
deck, or in the dining salon, had a fair chance of rescue,
for the beach and anxious rescuers were close at hand.
Those who were still asleep in their staterooms had little
chance. The ship struck at 8:26 a. m. There was no tremendous shock to throw the sleepers from their berths,
just the screech of tortured metal and the quick loss of
way. At 8:28 the ship was beached. Many a sleepy passenger, awakened by the sound of the ship's striking
though still befuddled, had felt the renewed thump of
the screw as the Captain drove for the shore, and merely
turned over for another wink or two of Sunday morning
sleep. At 8:29 the boats were being lowered, the ship's
back was broken, the masts were fallen, the bridge and
the Captain were catapulted overboard, and most of the
stateroom doors were jammed immovably shut. At 8:30
the *California* lay fathoms deep under the blue waters of
Gambier Bay.

Some of the late sleepers saved themselves or were
saved by crewmen—and crew women—of particular courage. Stewardess Margaret Tracy smashed in doors and
pulled out a half dozen trapped passeengers in the 180
seconds of time that were allowed her.

Things could, of course, have been much worse. There
were 146 people aboard the steamer when she pulled out
from the dock at Gambier Bay. Just four minutes away
from the dock, she met disaster, in full view of a great
many people who had tugs and launches and rowboats
close at hand for rescue. One hundred and eleven of her
people were thus saved. But thirty-five were drowned.
That was one human life for each fathom the chart makers
erred when they marked the channel into Gambier Bay.
The big ships had not begun to call there until the year

before when the cannery was built. The coast survey crew that took the soundings there probably did not feel it worth while to spend much time in that isolated bay. They did not stay long enough to notice the huge pinnacle rock that bored toward the surface out in the channel. They marked thirty-five fathoms there too.

The Alaska Steamship Company's *Jefferson*, south bound, had picked up the *California's* S O S and turned about to give what help she could. She took the survivors and the few bodies she found to Juneau. There, those who wanted to go back Outside were put aboard the *Northwestern*, which reached Seattle with thirty-seven survivors and ten coffined bodies. Seven of the rescued passengers stayed in a Juneau hospital. The rest pressed on north to the gold fields. Twenty-seven of the dead stayed in the dark, shattered staterooms, their late Sunday morning doze extended into eternity. On the shores of Gambier Bay the Indians pulled many cases of whiskey from the water and got very drunk.

Some time later a survey ship was dispatched to make a new chart of the waters that were the grave of the *State of California,* for, as Captain Cann said after his ship was lost:

"When a chart is incorrect, it is much, much worse than none at all."

IT WAS FIVE O'CLOCK on the morning of August 26, 1914, and the ocean fog had drifted in from the North Pacific to lie in a dank pall over all of Puget Sound. Shore lights were all blotted out. From Olympia to Cape Flattery, ships felt their way by dead reckoning and the muted crying of fog horns on the points and capes.

Outward bound from Seattle to Alaska, the Pacific Coast Steamship Company's liner *Admiral Sampson* groped her way down Admiralty Inlet under a dead-slow bell, the resonant voice of her whistle wailing sadly at brief intervals. In the dimly-lit pilothouse, Captain Zim Moore and Pilot Peter Obert kept anxious watch. Wraiths of fog, drifting in through the open windows, filled the pilothouse with the marshy smell of early morning sea mist. The two men listened intently to the small

169

sounds around them: the gentle, almost inaudible chuckle of water at the ship's stem, the monotonous drip of congealed fog, the hiss of surplus steam at the stack safeties, and the faint echo of the horns and whistles on distant ships and lighthouses. Every sixty seconds these small sounds were snuffed out in the hoarse vibration of their own siren, close above their heads. As they heard the great reed horn on Point No Point grow louder through the muffled fog, they prepared to change course to round the invisible headland.

Far ahead now they discerned the ghostly hooting of another steamer's siren. With the passing minutes this grew nearer and louder. From a distant echo of sound it fast developed into a strident warning of disaster. Captain Moore turned inquiring eyes to the pilot, whose face was strained in the dim light of the binnacle. Both veteran seamen knew that the quickly rising volume of the on-coming ship's voice meant only one thing. She was travel-ing at a dangerously high speed through the blinding mist that made the *Sampson's* fo'c'sle invisible from the pilot-house.

"She must be doing eighteen knots! And in this . . . " the Captain's words were swallowed by the tremendous yell of the other ship's siren. The wet insulation of fog had made it hard to determine her exact position before, but now there could be no doubt. She was just off the port bow—on a collision course.

Captain Moore wrenched open the pilothouse door to go where his seaman's instinct took him, the point of greatest danger, the ship's port bridge wing. The *Samp-son's* whistle blasted out in answer to the onrushing stranger. The pilot leaped to the wheel to add his strength to his order "Hard a'starboard!" The engine room tele-graph clanged from dead slow, three knots, to "Full a'stern!" Far below, the engines stopped with a tired sigh of steam, then pounded into action again with the liquid thunder of a reversed screw.

But it was too late. Out of the void ahead loomed the slender steel prow of the three-stacked Canadian Pacific express liner *Princess Victoria*. A great bow wave curled from her forefoot and black smoke streaked aft from her tall, buff funnels. The Clyde-built *Princess* boats held a tight schedule on their triangular run between Vancouver, Victoria, and Seattle, their skippers priding themselves on keeping the line's sailing schedule unbroken and little caring what else got broken in the process. Towboat skippers learned to keep the *Princess* liners in mind along with such other navigation hazards as reefs, tide rips and storm warnings. When they heard one of the arrogant sisters roaring and ramping down the foggy Sound, they would, like pygmies scattering from a charging elephant, cut their barges or log rafts loose to run for shallow water.

Being a deep-water ship, the *Sampson* could not pursue such tactics even if there had been time, and there was no time. At three knots she barely had steerage way. Nothing could be done to avoid the onrushing *Princess*. The sharp steel bows of the Canadian liner knifed through the fog to bite deep into the Admiral liner's green hull on the port side, just abaft the beam. The three thousand tons of speeding steel cut the *Sampson* almost in two. No sooner had the rending crash of the first impact subsided than a new terror faced the shocked passengers and crew of the mortally-wounded Alaska steamer. Fuel oil from the crushed tanks caught fire to light the scene of disaster with the sinister dance of flames.

In the few minutes left to them, the officers and crewmen of both ships lived up to the best traditions of the sea. The *Princess Victoria's* boats took to the water with the precision of men-of-war. Within minutes they were transferring passengers from the sinking liner to the safety of the *Princess's* decks. Captain Hickey kept his steamer's bow pressed deep in the *Sampson's* side until the fire from the burning tanks and the downward pressure of the foundering ship forced him to reverse his engines.

As the *Princess* backed away from the *Sampson,* the people of both ships saw a screaming human torch clinging to the scorched wreckage at the Canadian liner's bow. A stowaway had hidden himself away below decks on the *Sampson* before she left Seattle. The crushing blow of the other ship had trapped him there in the jagged steel and flaming oil until the bow was withdrawn. In a few moments he lost his hold to drop to a quick and merciful death in the misty waters.

The ships had met off Point No Point at 5:45 a. m. Within twelve minutes the *Admiral Sampson* was under seventy fathoms of water. The splendid discipline of both crews was all that kept this from becoming one of the worst marine disasters in the Northwest's history.

Captain Moore, the Admiral liner's master, was on his first voyage after a long spell ashore. Although he had served as United States Marshal at Unga, Alaska, for several years, he proved that he had not forgotten his trade during his time on the beach. Calmly, as if docking his ship in some safe harbor, he directed the lowering of the boats and the transfer of the passengers. Pilot Obert stayed at the wheel until the pilothouse was blown overboard by the rush of compressed air from the ruptured hatches. Quartermaster Marquist remained at his Captain's side on the listing steamer's bridge. In the wireless room, chief operator Walter Recker crouched grimly over his key to keep the liner's frantic distress call crackling through the foggy air. Farther down the straits the *Admiral Watson* heard her sister ship's S O S and smoke blossomed at her stack as the fire room crowded on steam in answer to the clanging call of the telegraph, "Full speed ahead!" Ignoring the wailing warnings of the fog horns, she raced toward the scene of disaster.

Before she got there the *Sampson* was gone. Captain Moore, the faithful quartermaster still at his side, went down at his post on the bridge. The radio operator kept the blue spark jumping on his set until a dark mass of water swept him into oblivion; and the antenna, high up between the masts, slipped beneath the surface. Below decks the chief engineer was trying to pull an unconscious woman passenger from the twisted wreckage of her cabin when the world was blotted out in the ship's final plunge. These four men of great courage died with their ship in the company of eight others who, trapped in the wreckage or lost and panic stricken below decks, could not be saved in the few desperate minutes between the ramming and the sinking.

The international boundary line, which bisects the Straits of Juan de Fuca and Admiralty Inlet, makes a handy sanctuary for ships in legal difficulties. American vessels have been known to sneak across the line into American waters to escape the processes of Canadian civil law. Canadian ships have done the same act in reverse. This time the Pacific Coast Steamship Company took no chances. No sooner had the *Princess Victoria* landed the *Admiral Sampson's* survivors at her Seattle pier than she was boarded by a United States Marshal who proceeded to tack a libel notice on her pilothouse door. The slim *Princess* was imprisoned at the dock until such time as the Admiral Line's claim for close to a million dollars' damages was straightened out.

When the claim was finally cleared, the *Princess* liner, with a repaired bow, lived to plow the waters of the inland sea for many more years. But, if she had learned her lesson and slowed down any in the fog, it was not noticed by the cursing Mosquito Fleet skippers, who continued, like harried quail, to dash for shelter at her approach.[1]

1.—Few of the Puget Sound passenger steamers observed the speed regulations, the captains justifying their rapid navigation of invisible waterways as follows:

The companies demanded that schedules be maintained. If a skipper rang down the engines every time he encountered fog he would be on the beach with a new skipper speeding through the fog on his ship.

It was really more dangerous to slow down than to keep going. Courses, currents and tide sets are figured at the ship's normal cruising speed.

THE *Princess Maquinna* is a single-screw steel steamship of seventeen hundred gross tons, built at Victoria in 1913. Commanded by Captain Edward Gillam, she maintained a regular freight and passenger service between Victoria and other Vancouver Island ports, flying the Canadian Pacific's checkerboard house flag.

With a full cargo and a heavy passenger list she put out from Tofino on Thanksgiving Day, 1915, bound as usual for Victoria. November had been a month of hurricanes and smashing seas across the whole vast expanse of the Pacific and much damage had been done to shipping. The big freighter *Robert Dollar* had clawed past Cape Flattery with one propeller blade gone, torn off by the racing engines' vibration in the lift of the moun-

174

tainous seas. The *Shintsu Maru* made it with her poop
swept clean, lifeboats, davits and rails gone, and holds
smashed in. Outbound steamers met 87-miles-an-hour
winds, and some of them made Honolulu in distress. As
the *Princess Maquinna* left the shelter of the harbor and
put out to sea, she faced the full force of one of these
howling Pacific storms.

Captain Gillam, a careful seaman, remarked to his
mate that this was the worst storm he had seen in four-
teen years of coasting the treacherous Graveyard. Looking unhappily over the gray-waste of steep, foam-crested
ridges and the spouting rocks to port, the mate fully
agreed. The Captain was preparing to put his ship
about and run back for shelter when the lookout reported
a vessel on the port bow, close in to the breakers. Through
their binoculars the steamer's officers made her out to
be a full-rigged ship with most of her spars bare and both
anchors out. As they drew closer they could see that she
was a huge iron ship with some of her dark, sodden sails
fluttering wildly in tattered streamers. Finally they saw
the ragged wisp of a Chilean ensign flying upside down
from the peak signal halyards. There could be no further
doubt that the big square-rigger was in distress. As if to
clinch the matter, a rocket flared from her afterdeck to
burst in the storm rack above.

The *Princess Maquinna* responded bravely to the call
for help. Although the wind was fast rising to hurricane
force from the southeast, while vicious seas were sweeping
clear across her bridge, she edged slowly ahead and inshore toward the anchored ship. Though she flew the
Chilean flag and the name *Carelmapu* could be made out
on her rounded counter, the battered windwhip looked
familiar to Captain Gillam. She was, indeed, the old
British *Kinross,* Liverpool built and sold to the South
Americans in her old age.

Within two hundred yards of the Chilean, the *Princess
Maquinna's* anchor was dropped; ten fathoms of chain

clanked out from the windlass. Her passengers and crew saw men on the sailing ship's deck lower a boat, fill it with men, and head for the steamer's lee. In a few moments they lowered another boat. It looked as if the windship men might make it safely to the shelter of the steamer's deck.

But at that moment the wind suddenly whipped around to the southeast to come screaming in at seventy-five miles an hour. Captain Gillam, almost swept from the bridge by the first tremendous gust, clung desperately to the rail as he looked astern. A truly giant wave, tall as a five-story building, rose hissing toward them, blotting out the sky. That great hurricane gust and the monstrous wave that rode its tail ended all thought or hope of rescue.

As the steamer spiraled up fifty feet to the thrust of the comber, a ripping crash sounded forward. With unbelieving eyes, the Captain saw the ponderous steel winch rise upward from the deck to vanish overside, with chain and anchor still intact. Now it was a fine question whether he could keep his own ship off the rocky fangs to leeward, but as he turned to get the steamer underway he saw the great wave complete its work of destruction. It simply overwhelmed the first of the laboring boats from the *Carelmapu,* blotting it out under tons of crashing water. The other it tossed back against the ship's iron hull and literally ground to sawdust, boat and crew together. Then it broke over the ship and swept her deck clean of men and gear. Both anchor chains snapped and the vessel swung broadside on the waiting rocks. When another comber crashed against her side, she was hurled across the rocky reef, her towering masts gone overside in a mass of splintered spars and tangled rigging. Within minutes, the tall, proud ship had been reduced to a battered ruin, mastless, torn, and helpless in the Graveyard's grip.

But before the scud and driven sleet blotted out the

melancholy sight, those on the *Princess Maquinna* saw that
there was still human life aboard the crumpled hulk.
Three figures could be made out on the poop. One,
dressed in black oilskins, clung to the ship's wheel, as if
he still hoped to pilot her away from the grim shore that
was pounding her to pieces beneath his feet.

There was no hope for the huddled group on the wreck
and when the *Princess* liner arrived at Victoria, her
captain reported the Chilean ship *Carelmapu* lost with
all hands on the west coast of Vancouver Island. Later
it was found that five of the ship's company of twenty-five
had escaped. The hurricane had continued to force the
wreck ashore, and the ebbing tide had left her high and
dry. Then Captain Fernando Desolmes, three crewmen
and a young passenger crawled from the tangled wreckage
and made their way to land.

Later, Captain Desolmes told what happened:

"We arrived off Cape Flattery early on Wednesday morning
and passed that point five times, signaling for a tow boat. We
were within a half mile of Flattery but apparently no one saw us.
After laying in the strait all day, we were caught in a southeast
gale and beaten up the coast of Vancouver Island. As we passed
Pachena Point some of our canvas was stripped and I made
distress signals. The velocity of the wind drove the *Carelmapu*
within one mile of Leonard Island Lighthouse. When I sighted
the steamer I dropped both anchors in 240 fathoms, but the wind
changed to the southwest and the chains broke. We were inbound from Caleta Buenas, Chile to Puget Sound, via Honolulu."

The *Princess Maquinna* got a patch to cover the gaping
hole on her fo'c'sle and a new winch to replace the one
torn on her like a rotten tooth by the mighty breaker that
killed the *Carelmapu*. Then she went back to her routine
coasting duties, but those who were with her on that
day never forgot Thanksgiving, 1915, when they watched
helplessly while twenty men and a stately ship died on
Gowland Rocks.

THE NORTHWEST CORNER OF AMERICA has had its full share of shipwreck and disaster. A few of these tragedies stand out as melancholy classics—the loss of the *Pacific,* the stranding of the *Valencia,* and the sinking of the Puget Sound steamers *Clallam* and *Dix*—but none has achieved the grim fame of the Canadian Pacific liner *Princess Sophia.*

Not only was the loss of life far greater than in any of the other wrecks; there was the added, bitter knowledge that no one need have perished. In most marine disasters there is the fatalistic consolation that everything possible was done to save the victims from the sea, or that the ship was overwhelmed far from land where no help from human hands was possible. The *Princess Sophia* met her fate within a few yards of shore and all on board could easily have been saved, probably without even

178

Not all the ships that stranded on North Pacific shores were lost. The British ship *Kilbrainnan*, beached on Point Wilson in the 1890s, was salvaged.

The bark *Melanope*, given up for lost, returned to port.

The H_____ der steam schooner Saline Cruz (ex- Anne Hanify) burned off Grays Harbor in 1949. Thanks to radio and an getting their feet wet. But the chance was missed and no one who was aboard the liner on her last voyage lived to tell the story of her final hours.

By October of 1918, most of the young men of Alaska had joined the United States Army to help fight a war. A transport loaded with them sailed from Skagway early in the month, many of their families planning to follow them in the *Princess Sophia* to spend the war years on the Outside. The Canadian liner was scheduled to leave Skagway, at the northern tip of the Inland Passage, on October 22. Scores of miners took the last river boats down the Yukon just before the ice closed in for the winter, making connections with the liner by train from White Horse. Also, many of the Yukon River steamboat men, their boats tied up for the winter, were going outside on the *Sophia*. Old prospectors, business men, pioneer women and their children, and a few belated operators from the scattered Army Signal Corps stations swelled the passenger list to 268. The crew of seventy-five brought the total number aboard at sailing time to 343 persons.

It was a gay scene at the dock as the *Princess Sophia* swung into the stream and started toward the channel. Many of the passengers had known months or years of loneliness in the Far North. Now they were headed to that fabulous place they called "Outside"—a land of bright lights, of glittering hotels and gliding motor cars, of movies and ice cream sodas. Children who had never seen but had often heard of these marvels were in a delirium of joy at the great adventure beyond.

Stack whistles blared out in vast pride and the bow wave creamed higher at the trim prow as the *Princess Sophia* swept smoothly down the sheltered waters of narrow Lynn Canal. Her course lay between majestic, ice-capped mountains streaked with glittering glacial streams. Juneau, somewhat more than a hundred miles ahead, was the first scheduled stop. Then the liner would steam on south, past the Alexander Archipelago, past the Queen

Charlotte Islands, through the Strait of Georgia, between Vancouver Island and the Canadian mainland, and into the harbor of Vancouver.

But four hours out of Skagway the Alaska winter caught up with the *Princess Sophia*. A blinding snowstorm swept in on an arctic wind. Below, gongs clanged and the engineer jumped to the steam valve. The flash of the great piston rods and outthrust eccentrics slowed to a solemn rhythm as the hiss of the bow wave subsided to a gentle murmur. With blasting whistle, the liner groped her way down the narrow fairway, alert officers on the bridge counting the seconds between the siren's hoarse bellow and the muted echoes from the invisible shores on either side.

In the black, pre-dawn hours on Thursday, the *Princess Sophia's* luck ran out. Bells jangled wildly in the engine room again; thundering screws bit deep to the thrust of reversed engines. But all the speed of desperation cannot make a 3,000-ton steamer halt quickly in her course. A jarring shudder swept along two thirds of the keel, the bow lifted high, and the big liner was hard aground on the rocks of Vanderbilt Reef, midway between Skagway and Juneau.

There was no panic; not even any great concern. The water was placid, the ship not pounding on the rocks. With the steam still up, the lights burned brightly in the cabins. The shock of the grounding had been so gentle that even the children were not frightened, just concerned at the delay in their trip to the magic land of Outside. The ship's wireless sent a call for help crackling out into the snowy blackness of the night. The full light of morning revealed the cheering sight of a buff-bowed steamer pushing white water and trailing black smoke as she raced toward the stranded liner. It was the U. S. lighthouse tender *Cedar*, with Captain J. W. Leadbetter. She was soon joined by the cable ship *Peterson*.

Captain Leadbetter was set to begin taking off the

Sophia's passengers, but the liner's master, Captain F. L. Locke, was in no hurry. It was still calm; his ship was setting well on the reef, solid and on an even keel. Canadian Pacific officials in Vancouver had radioed that the *Sophia's* sister ship, *Princess Alice,* along with a powerful salvage tug, had been dispatched to her assistance. The passengers were entirely at ease and might as well wait for the *Princess Alice.* Then they could go on to Vancouver in more comfort, without being subjected to the inconveniences of a lighthouse tender's scanty accommodations. In the meantime, Locke said it would be appreciated if the *Cedar* would stand by, just in case something *should* happen.

The *Cedar* stayed, but when something happened it was so fast that nothing could be done about it.

All was peaceful enough throughout Thursday night and Friday morning. The snow fell steadily, yet there was no wind to speak of, and the *Princess Sophia* continued to sit regally on her rocky throne, seemingly as solid as the granite shore so close alongside. But late in the day the snowstorm suddenly became a blizzard. Without warning, winds of hurricane force came shrieking down the rocky funnel of Lynn Canal and the quiet waters were suddenly whipped into hissing, 30-foot waves. Several ships standing by had to look to their own safety. Captain Leadbetter tried to bring the *Cedar* close to the stranded liner, and he got within four hundred yards of her, but the *Cedar's* anchors were dragging and she was being swept fast toward the snarling, spouting reef that had impaled the *Princess* liner. It would do her people no good to have the lighthouse tender join them there, so the *Cedar* beat her way back into the channel.

Aboard the liner there was still no panic. She was taking a beating now; still two thirds of her 300-foot hull was firmly imbedded on the reef, and chances were good that she would stay there. The solid shore a few yards away gave a certain false sense of security. Since no

boats could be launched in the maelstrom around the
ship, the beach might as well have been a thousand
miles away.

During the black night of the twenty-fifth, the hurricane reached a howling climax and the wireless operator
on the *Cedar* picked up a message from the *Princess
Sophia*. She had been driven across the reef and was
sinking. Through the blinding snow the *Cedar* raced at
full speed, the beam of her searchlight making a white
cone of slanting snow ahead of her. But the *Princess
Sophia* was no longer on her rocky throne, and since
there was no way of telling where she had gone, nothing
could be done. On Saturday morning a message went
out from the U. S. Wireless Station at Juneau:

"*Princess Sophia* driven across reef last night. No survivors.
75 in crew, 268 passengers. Everything possible was done. Terrible
weather prevailed."

The *Cedar* returned to Vanderbilt Reef at dawn, but
just the foremast of the stricken liner protruded from the
water. The storm had done its work and the wind was
dying down. Four capsized lifeboats rose and fell sluggishly on the choppy, gray water. Only one body, that of
a woman, was sighted from the tender's bridge.

Then the *Cedar's* wireless tapped out the message that
ended all hope:

"No sign of life. No hope of survivors."

After that the bodies began to come ashore. For thirty
miles the beaches were lined with the dead and with
the sodden and pitiful things that had been precious
enough for them to take on the long journey Outside—
clothing and books and faded photographs, and the
broken toys of the children who never saw the wonderful
world beyond that had been promised them.

Most of the bodies were fully clothed, with life jackets
strapped on. It appeared that discipline and order had

prevailed until the end. Many had watches with the hands stopped at seven-thirty. The liner's radio operator had been in contact with the *Cedar* until eight the night before and it was assumed that the *Princess Sophia* had taken her final plunge close to seven-thirty on Saturday morning, shortly before the lighthouse tender arrived on the scene.

No one will ever know for sure. No one lived to tell.

IN THE RARE, early spring which came to the Northwest Coast toward the latter part of March, 1921, the big two-stacker *Governor*, pride of the Admiral Line, made a fast and pleasant voyage up the coast. On the morning of March 31, she passed the guardian rock, Tatoosh, and made her 180-degree swing to starboard, into the Straits of Juan de Fuca. With the jagged rocks of Flattery and the bleak lee shore of the Graveyard astern, her voyage from San Francisco to Seattle was as good as over; a brief stop at Victoria, then the last hundred miles over placid inland waters to her pier and a quick turn-around for the return voyage south. Her 172 passengers were prepared to enjoy their last day and night aboard ship, looking forward to the farewell dance to be held that evening.

184

A father and mother, with their two little girls, stood at the boat-deck rail to starboard as the *Governor* swept past Neah Bay. This was home to them, for the father, W. W. Washburn, was an employe of the Neah Bay Indian Agency. First to spy the white spot among the somber fir trees was eight-year-old Sadie. This was the only glimpse they had of their shore-side cottage. As the steamer sped on toward Victoria they laughed over this joke— they were already more than home!

But the liner did not stop at Neah Bay. The little family had to go on to Seattle, where they would board a smaller Sound steamer for the trip back. Father was not at all sure that Sadie had picked out the right house, but Mother and the two girls were positive they had seen home quite clearly. Anyhow, they never saw it again.

The *Governor* cleared Victoria and the farewell dance was a success. It ended just before midnight and the orchestra put up their instruments while most of the passengers drifted down to the staterooms to bed. In a midship cabin stateroom on the starboard side, Mrs. Washburn had long since tucked Sadie and ten-year-old sister Jane into their berths.

As the closing minutes of the month ticked off, Pilot Tom Martin stood by the quartermaster in the wheelhouse, watching the flashing light on Point Wilson, off the starboard bow. Far ahead he could make out the green flash of the light on the dim point of Marrowstone Island and, miles to port, the dark, lonely bulk of Whidbey Island. No ships' lights were reflected on the calm surface of Admiralty Inlet ahead, but off to starboard he saw the masthead lights of a freighter standing out from Port Townsend. The two ships sighted each other when they were two miles apart, and they never lost sight of each other. The freighter was the *West Hartland,* owned by the U. S. Shipping Board, but also operated by the Pacific Steamship Company—the Admiral Line. Outbound from Port Townsend to Bombay, she

had the right of way and Captain John Alwen held his
course.

Aboard the *Governor* eight bells struck midnight, the
beginning of the first day of April. In the pilothouse
the watch changed but pilot Martin remained in charge
of the ship. With plenty of sea room and ample time
safely to cross the freighter's bows, the passenger liner
kept her speed.

Suddenly the illusion of safety, fashioned of drifting
wraiths of mist and darkness, was gone. In the gloom the
red port light of the *West Hartland* glowed like a
malevolent eye. There was no more sea room as the
bellowed warning of her siren shattered the night. In
the *Governor's* wheel house the quartermaster spoked
the wheel hard to port; the pilot's hand slammed the engine room telegraph to *stop engines,* then to *full astern.*
Steam spurted at her forward funnel in a series of short,
desperate whistle blasts.

In the keeper's house at Point Wilson Light, Captain
Thomas heard the disaster call of the *Governor.* As he
pushed up a window and looked out to sea, the hands of
the clock stood at four minutes past twelve. He was in
time to see the high steel bow of the *West Hartland* knife
far into the side of the careening liner.

Down in a midship stateroom on the starboard side,
Mrs. Washburn awakened from a dream of home to a
nightmare of reality. The great prow of the freighter
crashed through the liner's side and through the stateroom wall in a twisted mass of steel and wooden wreckage. Sadie and Jane had been swept out of sight, engulfed
while they slept and pinned somewhere in that wreckage.

The *West Hartland's* master wisely kept his ship's bow
pressed into the gaping wound in the *Governor's* side, his
engines turning over slow ahead. Because the freighter's
stem plugged the death wound it had inflicted, the liner
stayed afloat for an hour and eleven minutes, while most
of the passengers and crew clambered across onto the

freighter's bow, or leaped overboard and were hauled in by the *Hartland's* crew. Then the freighter backed slowly off and the S. S. *Governor,* pride of the Pacific Coast fleet, was finished.

As always, when disaster strikes at sea, there were courageous spirits who cheered the frightened and helped the weak. Such was the *Governor's* cook. With white teeth flashing in his black face, Chef Bodkin joked with crying children while he helped stow them safely in lifeboats. When a fur-clad dowager bewailed the loss of her jewels, the old negro told her, "Ma'am, you ain't got troubles. Think of that new suit I bought in Frisco . . . Suit, ah bids you one last farewell." People laughed then; and since panic cannot start where there is laughter, the *Governor's* cook probably earned hero rating that black midnight off Marrowstone.

As the dying liner sank lower in the water there was a rending explosion. The hull jackknifed, breaking in two in the middle. Bow and stern lifted high in the misty darkness, then plunged downward and were gone from sight. Eight souls went down with the ship—three crew members and five passengers.

In a shattered stateroom amidships on the starboard side, two small girls, trapped in their twisted berths, were included in that final, awful plunge, but they were not alone. Because she could not get them out, their mother stayed with them. All three went home together after all.

SINCE THE FIRST RECORDED shipwreck there in 1792, the famous Inland Passage of Alaska has claimed a long list of ships stranded, sunk and gone missing. Stranded there that year were Vancouver's exploration ships *Discovery* and *Chatham*. The two British naval vessels were saved with a minimum of damage, but many of those that followed were less fortunate. The 1,000-mile waterway from Seattle to Skagway is almost a continuation of the sheltered reaches of Puget Sound; a deep channel, protected from the sweep of the North Pacific by the hundreds of great and small islands that guard its seaward flank. When fog and storm are absent, the way is as safe as a broad and gentle river; but when the Inland Passage is blanketed in mist, or the snow drives down the narrow channel on the wings of an

188

arctic blizzard to make a ship's bow invisible to the
bridge, then there is danger.

The Inland Passage was, until recent years, unguarded
by lighthouses or lifesaving ships or stations. A few
revenue cutters patrolled the northern waters; but, since
they bumped their snouts against rocks and draped
themselves over reefs as often as the privately-owned
ships,[1] they were seldom able to arrive in time to do any
good when disaster struck. Not a single lighthouse was
constructed in Alaskan waters until 1902.

The greatest dread of the northern seamen, though,
was the myriad of uncharted pinnacle rocks and sunken
reefs which beset the Passage. Submerged rock cones were
the more dangerous, for the reefs were fairly easy to lo-
cate and, under normal conditions, to avoid. A pinnacle
rock might lie in an area where soundings showing deep
water had been made on all sides and clear sailing indicated on the charts. Scores of ships might brush past
the lurking underwater trap safely; then an unlucky one,
a few yards more to port or starboard, be murdered by
the hidden fang of stone. Other pinnacles lay deep
enough to be passed over safely until an unusually low
tide. If a deeply-laden ship arrived at an unlucky moment
she was likely to be impaled on a hitherto unsuspected
rock. Not until the First World War period were drag
surveys begun to find and chart those hidden menaces.

The Inland Passage of Alaska is comparatively well
marked and well charted now, but no way has been discovered to dispel the clinging fogs or blinding snow
storms. Even with the elaborate present-day aids to
navigation, things sometimes go wrong; the mortality rate
of Alaska ships has always been high. Perhaps for this
reason new steamers are seldom built especially for that

1.—The revenue steamers *Wayanda* and *Lincoln* seldom made a cruise to
Alaska without striking a rock. In 1879, treasury agent Morris said, "The U. S. S.
Saginaw struck several times while in Alaska waters. The U. S. S. *Suwanee*
was lost on a sunken rock at the entrance to Queen Charlotte Sound, July 9,
1868, with great loss of life."—*Washington Historical Quarterly,* January, 1916.

trade. Old ships that have served for years on more conventional seas are brought west in their old age [2] to run the exotic Inland Passage. Such a ship was the S. S. *Yukon* of the Alaska Steamship Company. Built on the East Coast as the *Mexico,* she was later renamed *Colon,* running between New York and the Isthmus of Panama in pre-canal days. In 1926, she entered the Alaska trade. She was an elderly ship, twenty-seven years old, when she took up her new duties in the Far Northwest, but she stayed on the Alaska run without a fatal mishap for another twenty years.

On Sunday evening, February 3, 1946, the old *Yukon* pulled out of Seward on her last voyage. She was headed south for Seattle with a capacity load of passengers going Outside. Most of them were military personnel due for discharge at state-side army posts, or out on leave. Aboard were 148 soldiers headed for civilian life, another 132 soldiers traveling south on furlough, and 55 civilian passengers. The 125-man crew brought the total to 496. From the start the weather was nasty. Soon the *Yukon* was being pushed along by a bad storm, a typical blinding Alaskan blizzard.

Before midnight she was a lost ship, blindly groping her way toward disaster. On the snow-whipped bridge her officers and pilot listened to the hoarse bellow of the whistle above them, striving vainly to catch a familiar echo bounced back from the rocky cliffs. The swirling snow blanket distorted and muffled the echo. The screaming wind snatched the sound and flung it ahead into the darkness. On such a night there was nothing to guide the *Yukon.* Even when she struck, no one knew where she was, only that she was hard and fast aground, helpless,

2.—A classical example is the ancient Cunarder *Parthia,* iron-hulled propeller built for the plush North Atlantic passenger trade. Renamed *Victoria,* she was brought to the West Coast before the Alaska Gold Rush, serving as an Alaska passenger liner until just before the Second World War. In the spring of 1951, "Old Vic" entered her eighty-first year of service.

and lashed by 20-foot waves that swept icy spray clear
across her decks. The old ship had crashed ashore a
little after midnight. The gray, snow-choked dawn revealed the hopelessness of her situation. She lay, bow in,
on a narrow, rocky, foam-lashed beach, from which rose
tremendous cliffs to lose themselves in the white void far
above the trucks of the *Yukon's* masts.

It was early on Monday morning, February 4, that the
first S O S went out from the doomed ship. Captain
Chris Trondsen gave his ship's approximate position, reporting that she was hard aground, with the engine room
and No. 3 hold flooded. After that the people aboard the
Yukon could only wait while the wonderful modern lifesaving forces of the coast guard, the navy and the army
swung into action.

From Cordova the coast guard cutter *Onandaga* raced
under forced draft toward the disaster scene. The big
navy tug *Curb* followed in her wake. Two army mine-
sweepers were dispatched to the scene. A train loaded
with medical supplies and first-aid workers, having received rights over everything on the Alaska Railroad,
roared down from Anchorage to Seward to be ready for
the survivors. Planes were ordered to Seward to evacuate
any seriously injured victims to army base hospitals.

Just as darkness was falling, the *Onandaga* reached the
bleak beach where the passenger liner lay. Her searchlights pierced the falling snow to spotlight the stricken
liner, while her boats fought through the great seas to
take off the first of the women and children. Children
were carried down cargo nets draped over the stranded
ship's side and stowed safely in the tossing surfboats.
Their mothers followed them down the frozen nets. The
Onandaga, slowly working in closer to the wreck, shot
lifelines across the *Yukon's* listing deck. As the night
wore on, the wind and snow died down, the temperature
dropping below freezing. Everything became glazed with
ice—ships, lines, small boats—but the rescue operations

went on. The cutter *Cedar* came foaming in to join the *Onandaga*. The *Curb* swung in, and the army ships.

The ice-sheathed bulk of the *Yukon* stood out starkly in the glare of the many searchlights, while the sea spouted against the mile-high background of bleak mountain heights. During that first night on the beach the *Yukon* received her ultimate deathblow. Some sea, angrier than the rest, struck the old hull, already weakened by a thousand vicious blows. In a great rending of wrenched steel and broken rivets, the ship broke in two. As the passengers who were still aboard raced for the safety of the forward section, the stern lifted, rolled far to starboard, then slipped out of sight beneath deep water. Roger Bassette, ship's clerk, was one who failed to make it forward as the stern twisted off and sank. He was lucky, though, and lived to tell about it. Here is what he said:

"I saw some of my buddies washed overboard a few minutes before I was thrown into the water myself. Everybody had been ordered to move toward the bow half of the ship, which remained firmly wedged on the rocks, but some of us didn't make it. Thank God we had on lifebelts."

Many of those spilled off the broken stern half of the liner, like Bassette, were pulled to safety. For several days thereafter, the coast guard reported no known casualties, but the final count recorded eleven persons, five civilians and six soldiers, swept off the *Yukon's* stern and lost in the icy water. That was the full death toll of the *Yukon* disaster—eleven dead out of a total ship's company of 496. Had the wreck occurred a few years earlier, before the days of high speed, streamlined rescue techniques, the casualty list would have been much higher. Even as it was, there were loud cries of inefficiency and cowardice on the part of the *Yukon's* officers and crewmen. But that came later. At the moment all were too cold and terrified to do much complaining.

At 10:30 a. m., Tuesday, Febraury 5, the first boatload of women and children, those rescued the night before by the boat crews from the *Onandaga,* arrived at
Seward. There the forty-seven blanket-wrapped, shiver-
ing women and children learned something of Alaskan
kindness. The whole town had turned out to take care
of them. Private homes were opened to them. They were
given clothes and warm blankets and hot food and, most
important of all to the cold, exhausted women and children, warm human friendship and compassion. The
coastguardsmen had done their best; hairy, tattooed
ships' cooks had warmed milk and stirred formulas while
other ratings changed diapers and rocked the frightened,
pinch-faced babies until they became warm and sleepy.
But it was good to find sanctuary in a warm, bright home
on dry land with other women to care for the babies with
greater efficiency and less self-consciousness.

Newspapermen, of course, were at the dock to meet
the first survivors. They managed to interview some of
the victims before these were whisked away by the ladies
of the Red Cross Motor Corps. Their stories gave the
outside world its first clear picture of the *Yukon* disaster.

Through lips blue with cold and exhaustion, the survivors told of hellish experiences aboard the stricken S.
S. *Yukon.* Lashed throughout the day by gales, numbed
by ice, rocked by winds which swept 20-foot waves against
the 360-foot ship until she split in the middle, the first
arrivals smiled feebly at the first-aid men who met them
at Seward's docks.

Meantime, the ice-shrouded half ship was being rapidly cleared of the remaining passengers and crewmen.
Some escaped ashore by breeches buoy; others were taken
to the rescue ships by small boats and army landing
craft. When it was learned that a number of survivors
were apparently marooned at bleak Cape Fairfield, near
the wreck scene, a party of Alaska sourdoughs began the
trek across the snow-clogged mountains by dog sled to

rescue them. They had not counted on the versatile army landing barges, which were prepared to run ashore and remove those of the *Yukon's* company who were huddled there. But the old-timers made themselves useful by building snug shelters and roaring fires for the bedraggled shipwreck victims, while these waited for the seas to moderate and for the army craft to finish their job of transferring passengers from the *Yukon* to the rescue ships. Planes droned over the frozen, mile-high mountain to drop blankets and food and first-aid equipment to the huddled little group on the beach. All in all, they waited in comparative comfort.

The *Yukon* had sent out her first S O S at 6:09 a.m. on Monday morning. That night she broke in two. By Tuesday evening, 485 persons had been safely removed from the broken hulk. Only the eleven who were swept overboard as the after half of the ship careened and sank were lost. Rescue operations were conducted on a towering, rock-fanged lee shore in the face of a blizzard, huge seas and freezing cold.

But when the first of the *Yukon* survivors arrived at Seattle by plane they made some startling accusations. They said that the crew had broken into the bar stores when the ship struck the beach and had proceeded to get roaring drunk; that the officers had been unable to control the crew, had issued no orders, and had done nothing to safeguard the passengers; that crewmen had broken into and looted passengers' staterooms; and that only the bravery of the soldier passengers had prevented utter tragedy.

This made sensational news, the papers playing it up with big headlines. But these headlines were not so big or glaring when the bulk of the survivors arrived on the steamer *Alaska* to disprove most of the accusations.

Later arrivals told of many acts of kindness and bravery by the *Yukon* crew. A seaman had waded and swum into a flooded stateroom deep in the crumbling hull to find a pair of shoes for a small boy who would otherwise have gone barefoot down the freezing cargo nets to a small boat. A steward had waded to the galley in icy water up to his neck to get bottled water for a sick, thirsty baby.

The truth was probably about what it usually is in such cases. A few crew members probably got drunk. There was some thieving; to a few, disaster always seems a golden opportunity for plunder. An oiler from the *Yukon's* engine room perhaps made the acquaintance of the Seward jail when he tried to sell a pair of earrings to a jeweler who recognized them as a set he had made for a *Yukon* passenger. Likely it was the oiler and a few others like him who brought about the red-headlined shame that, for a while, surrounded the *Yukon* disaster. As sometimes happens, the drunkenness and dishonesty of a few bad men often overshadow the routine, honest courage of scores of good men.

So it probably was when the old *Yukon* made her voyage to the port of missing ships. But the screaming headlines of the day will be forgotten and the long list of the rescued will remain as the surest proof that American seamen are still worthy of the name, despite the very few whose evil ways still occasionally blacken—or redden—the front pages of newspapers.

WITH THE PASSING YEARS
the ships that sail the waters of the North Pacific have
changed much and so has the lot of the men who sail
with them. Seamen no longer have only their own
strength and skill to pit against the sea, nor do they pass
into the realm of complete mystery when they drop the
last smudge of land astern. The ship's voice, radio, is a
constant link with the world and, when disaster strikes,
an instantly-heeded cry for help. Electronic direction
finders have put an end to the old blind groping of "dead
reckoning," and through fog and darkness the sweeping
electronic eye of radar warns of hidden danger.

Ships have changed a great deal; the ocean not at all.
So, in spite of the best that science and human skill can
196

do, the ocean still claims her toll of ships and men. Still, the toll is much smaller now and most of the shipwrecks of the modern age are less sensational than the old-time disasters. There is a routine efficiency in the response to S O S calls that generally effects rescue operations with a minimum of delay and excitement, and a minimum loss of life. A good example was provided when, not long ago, the last of the steam schooners burned and sank off Grays Harbor.

The wooden steam schooners of the coast lumber trade were a breed of ships peculiar to the West Coast. The first of the tribe were little schooners of the conventional wind-driven type with modest steam engines shanghaied aboard to provide auxiliary power in case of adverse winds or sudden proximity to a lee shore. In time they evolved into a distinct kind of ship, with little resemblance to the old fore-and-afters from which they were descended. Wooden hulled and around two hundred feet long, they plied the coast in droves, hauling their cargoes of shingles, grape stakes, railroad ties, timber and rough logs between the ports of Washington, Oregon and California. Now they are an almost vanished race, seen as rarely as the sailing ships they supplanted, for the last one was built in 1923, and their mortality rate was high.

The steam schooners were particularly vulnerable to the hazards of the sea. Their wooden hulls loosened up with age so that they required constant pumping. They hugged the beach on their jaunts to the one-mill lumber ports and dog-holes, with the result that the fogs and gales of the Pacific frequently piled them up in the breakers. Their wooden hulls and oil-soaked bilges made them fire risks too, so that, all in all, the men of the steam schooner fleet—the Scandinavian Navy—were not good insurance ventures.

As steam schooners went, the *Anne Hanify* was a fairly modern ship, and bigger than most. She was built at

North Bend, Oregon, in 1920, and rated at 1,343 gross tons. In her later years she was sold to tramp around the West Coast, flying the Mexican tricolor at her blunt stern, her name changed to *Salina Cruz*. In the autumn of 1949, she put into Grays Harbor to load a full cargo of lumber, including a heavy deckload. Deep in the water, she crossed the bar on October 17, and headed for the open sea, a lonely remnant of the once-great fleet whose tall masts and booms had, a few years before, clustered at the docks of Aberdeen and Hoquiam. What happened to her in the following hours deserves mention for two reasons. Hers was probably the last steam schooner wreck on the West Coast, and she is a graphic example of how modern science saves lives at sea.

An inshore wind was kicking up as the *Salina Cruz,* ex-*Anne Hanify,* cleared the bar, and Captain Ivey kept her plunging westward, out to sea. Steam schooners needed plenty of sea room in a heavy blow and storm warnings were flying along the coast. By seven in the morning she had put 145 miles between herself and the surf-lashed Washington Coast. The wind was blowing twenty miles an hour when fire broke out in the engine room.

The worst possible danger threatened the men of the old wooden ship. Flames roared from the oil-soaked engine room to the dry upperworks and then to the lumber on the deck. In a short time the *Salina Cruz* was a blazing pyre, with the crew overside in the two lifeboats. The wind was still rising and the seas were growing heavier. If that had happened twenty years ago the crew would have had little chance of ever seeing land again.

But the *Salina Cruz* had a radio, and an S O S was transmitted before the "abondon ship" order was given. Fifty miles away, the U. S. Fish and Wildlife vessel *Black Douglas* picked up the disaster call and changed course to the steam schooner's last reported position. The coast guard picked up the S O S and swung into action. There was now no three-day wait for orders from

Washington by a leaky-boilered revenue cutter. Search
and rescue planes roared out over the stormy Pacific, soon
locating the pillar of smoke that marked the burning
ship. These circled the boats and kept the *Black Douglas*
informed of their position. The rescue ship was slowed
down by worsening weather. The wind was whooping in
at thirty miles an hour now and the seas were kicking
up accordingly. Big coast guard PBY's from Port Angeles swung into action, dropping emergency kits, signaling apparatus and rubber life rafts to the men in the
tossing boats. The coast guard cutters *Balsam* and *Bering
Strait* raced toward the scene, though the *Black Douglas*
was much closer. When lives are at stake, the modern
coast guard leaves nothing to chance; the *Black Douglas*
might develop engine trouble; then the other ships
would be needed.

A little after three o'clock in the afternoon the fiery
hulk of the old steam schooner rolled over in the heavy
seas to slide hissing beneath the surface. Fifteen minutes
later the water boiled and foamed as the hull reappeared,
broken in half and with the hundreds of thousands of feet
of lumber from her deckload spilled into the sea. By this
time the *Black Douglas* was only fifteen miles away; by
nightfall her searchlight had picked out the first lifeboat.
The ten men in it were taken off safely.

The other boat was in a worse plight. It was leaking
badly and was almost awash, but the plane-dropped flares
guided the *Douglas* to it an hour after the first boat was
picked up. The seven remaining survivors were hoisted
aboard and sent below to warm blankets and hot food.

Drifting timbers of the lost cargo were listed as a
menace to navigation until they broke up and drifted
ashore. The coast guard had to sink the broken halves of
the gutted ship, but no lives were lost in the last of the
steam schooner disasters.

Such rescue operations seem routine now, yet what

a miracle they would have been to the helpless victims of
the *Pacific* in 1873, or the *Valencia* in 1906, or to the
crews of the scores of windships that, in the old days,
went missing off the Northwest Coast, days when those
who went down to the sea in ships so often became helpless victims of the sea.

Of course the ocean still wins an occasional total victory. One of the North Pacific's most recent shipwrecks
proves this. The 455-foot Victory-type freighter *Pennsylvania* was a modern steel steamship with the most up-to-
date of navigational and communications equipment.
When she ran into trouble, her distress call was received
by the same efficient rescue agencies that had saved the
crew of the old steam schooner. But the *Pennsylvania*
was one of the unlucky ones; the treacherous northern
sea was too much for the puny efforts of men. Both ship
and crew suffered a disaster as complete as any in the
times before radio and coast guard and rescue planes.

The ill-fated *Pennsylvania* made a routine departure
from Seattle on January 5, 1952, bound for Yokohama,
Japan. She carried 6,000 tons of barley as well as general
cargo, the grain being transported to the Orient for the
Military Sea Transportation Service. Insofar as the rest
of the world knew, the freighter's voyage continued to be
routine for the next four days, as routine as any voyage
ever is when it begins in the teeth of a rising January gale
off Cape Flattery.

The first word that the ship was in danger came early
on the morning of January 9, when Captain George
Plover, the *Pennsylvania's* master, radioed that structural
failure of the vessel's hull was forcing him to put about
and attempt to return to Seattle. The ship was then some
450 miles west of the most northerly tip of Vancouver
Island. She was bucking a violent storm which was fast
growing worse.

Near noon more ominous tidings were flashed from the
doomed freighter. A 14-foot crack had opened down her

port side and smashing seas were rapidly filling her forward holds. All hands were reported "ready to abandon ship." When the S O S was received at Seattle, a search plane hurried out into the deep storm toward the position given by the ship's radio. It found no sign of the *Pennsylvania* or of her lifeboats.

Meanwhile, more terse messages came from the wallowing freighter. At 4:05 p. m., Captain Plover reported the steering gear, which had been smashed, as back in order; but the repairs were useless. The *Pennsylvania* had sunk so deep by the head that her rudder was completely out of water. At 4:22, another S O S flashed shoreward: "It looks like we have to abandon ship." Then, five minutes later, came the message: "Forty-five persons aboard. Four boats." At 4:30, the final two-word report was received: "Leaving now."

By the time the last message came through from the sinking freighter, early winter darkness had settled on the raging ocean. Nevertheless the rescue operations that had swung into action at noon were growing in strength. The strength of the storm was growing too. Through 45-foot waves plunged seven deep-sea ships toward the last position of the *Pennsylvania.* The Japanese steamship *Kimakawa Maru* was closest, but ships of many nations had joined the search — the Greek freighter *Cygnet III,* the Canadian frigate *Stonetown,* the U. S. Coast Guard cutter *Klamath,* the steamer *Shooting Star,* and the sea-going tugs *Hearthstone, Yocona* and *Island Sovereign.* Overhead in the storm rack, droned army, navy and coast guard planes. But there was no trace of the abandoned ship or of her crew.

The next day the hunt was widened. Canadian and American ships rolled and pitched on crisscross courses through the disaster area. More planes joined the search. Again not even a drifting spar or a smear of oil was sighted. As one coast guard pilot climbed wearily from his battered search plane, he voiced the feeling of most of those who had bucked the fury of the storm that had killed the *Pennsylvania*: "You can't imagine the size of those waves. I don't think those people had a chance."

Crewmen on a coast guard weather ship near the disaster area did not leave it to the imagination. They measured one of the great rollers as it swept in and found that it was nearly sixty feet from base to seething crown.

Despite the growing doubt that any could have survived the *Pennsylvania's* sinking, the search went on. Relieving planes came staggering out to take over the night watch, observers straining for a possible sight of flares from the sea below. They picked up only the range lights of the Japanese freighter and the Canadian frigate, both engaged in the surface hunt.

Day after day the search went on, growing in intensity even as hope grew dimmer. Twenty planes were scouring the seas on January 15, almost a week after the last message from the lost ship. Two of these aircraft sighted the only trace of the *Pennsylvania* that was ever found—a single battered lifeboat wallowing upside down in the trough of the now diminishing seas.

Four days later, the long search was called off; the plunging cutters turned toward their home stations and the planes were grounded.

And so a modern 7,800-ton steamship was listed as the latest victim of the angry North Pacific, the last hours of ship and crew cloaked in almost as complete a mystery as that of the old-time windships when they went missing. It may be that, like their ancestors, the Indians who live along the Graveyard's beaches will find the last clues in another enigma of the sea. Some wreckage from the broken ship may drift ashore there to add one more chapter to the mute story of the sea's incredible power.

———

Offshore the great steel ships come and go and the sleek, cruising cutters patrol their beats. The gray amphibians of the coast guard drone high above the sweeping eyes of the lighthouses and the coast beacons, while unseen beams of radio and radar knife through fog and darkness. The ocean may smile, as it did for Ferdinand Magellan when he gave it that deceptive name *Pacific*. But it changes quickly. And always the Graveyard broods on the horizon waiting to take final charge of man's next offering to the sea.

BIBLIOGRAPHY

READERS WHO MAY BE STIMULATED
by the samples offered herein to delve into the somber
but fascinating history of Pacific Northwest maritime
disasters will find themselves faced with limited material.
There is, of course, that bulky though indispensable
volume, *Lewis and Dryden's Marine History of the Pacific Northwest,* edited by E. W. Wright in 1896. Compiled at a time when many of the very early pioneers of
Northwest navigation were available to offer firsthand
source material, it gives thorough coverage to all phases
of the region's maritime history through the year 1895.
Although long out of print and almost worth its weight
in plutonium when found in a secondhand book store, it
is available in most of the larger libraries of Washington
and Oregon. It is a *must* for anyone seriously interested
in the shipping history of America's last frontier.

Unfortunately this ambitious volume bankrupted its
publishers and no one has seen fit to carry the work forward to the present day. Much of the research for this
book, therefore, took place in the newspaper files at the
Washington State Library at Olympia. The annual publication of the United States Department of Commerce,
Merchant Vessels of the United States, lists all shipping
losses of American vessels. A long list of names and dates
was culled from these books; then this list was checked
against the contemporary reports of the daily newspapers.
Much colorful material was gleaned in this manner, and
it is available to anyone with access to a library which
maintains files of old newspapers. It would be a waste of
space to record here the exact issues used to gather the
material in these stories, since the dates of the papers
correspond closely to the dates of the shipwrecks themselves, but it might be mentioned that the best coverage
of marine news of this region is to be found in the Seattle

Times and *Post-Intelligencer,* the Tacoma *Ledger* and *News-Tribune,* the Portland *Oregonian* and the San Francisco *Chronicle.*

The weekly trade magazine, *Marine Digest,* published in Seattle, is also an authoritative reference source covering approximately the past quarter century.

A number of fine books which do not deal primarily with the subject of shipwrecks will be found to contain interesting chapters or passages on the subject. Archie Binns, who is at his best when writing of the sea, tells of the destruction of the mystery ship off Port Gamble in his *Northwest Gateway,* which also contains the tragic story of the *Governor* and much other sea lore. His classic *Lightship,* while listed as a novel, will be important to anyone who has read this far in this book.

An excellent chapter on marine disasters appears in James G. McCurdy's *By Juan de Fuca's Strait,* long out of print but now available in a new edition. R. H. Calkins' history of the port of Seattle, *High Tide,* is full of tales of strandings and disasters, including the weird saga of the Japanese fishing boat which carried its dead crew to the coast of Washington.

Background and source material for the earliest days of American and European navigation of Pacific Northwest waters is found in Washington Irving's *Astoria* and and Edmond S. Meany's *Vancouver's Discovery of Puget Sound,* both classics in their field and both out now in new editions.

Cheechako into Sourdough, the autobiography of Thomas Wiedemann, contains a detailed and fascinating account of one particularly colorful shipwreck, that of the historic side-wheeler *Eliza Anderson,* while on an ill-starred voyage to the Klondike gold diggings. And, of course, James A. Gibbs's *Pacific Graveyard* and *Tillamook Light* need no introduction to Pacific Northwest shipwreck enthusiasts.

Kalmbach Publishing Company's general circulation

magazine, *Ships and the Sea,* contains frequent fact articles concerning marine disasters. It was from this source that permission was granted to reprint the story of Captain F. G. Lewis's adventures with the stern-wheeler *Victorian,* which first appeared in *Ships and the Sea,* and its 1953 annual, *True Sea Adventures.*

And to those loyal readers who are still with him, the author humbly mentions *Ships of the Inland Sea,* born on the same typewriter as *S O S North Pacific,* and including accounts of some Puget Sound shipwrecks not detailed in this later book.

GORDON R. NEWELL

INDEX

209

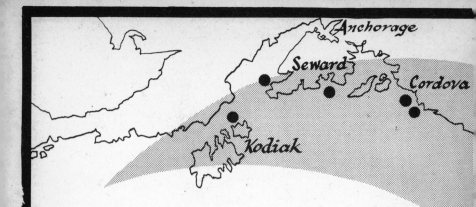

Anchorage

Seward

Cordova

Kodiak

TYPES OF MASTS

1. FOREMAST   4. SPANKERMAST
2. MAINMAST   5. JIGGERMAST
3. MIZZENMAST   6. PUSHERMAST

SKYSAILS
ROYALS
TOPGALLANTS
TOPSAILS
COURSES

FORE AND
AFT SAIL

SQUARE
SAIL

SLOOP   TWO MAST SCHOONER   THREE MAST SCHOONER   FOUR MAST SCHOONER

FIVE MAST SCHOONER   SIX MAST SCHOONER   BRIGANTINE

STEAM SHIP   FISH TRAWLER   TUG BOAT

 MAJOR DISASTER AREA